Writings on Philosophy and Economy of Power

Peter Herrmann

God, Rights, Law and a Good Society

Overcoming Religion and Moral as Social Policy Approach in a
Godless and Amoral Society

Writings on Philosophy and Economy of Power Vol. 2

EHV)

Herrmann, Peter

God, Rights, Law and a Good Society
Overcoming Religion and Moral as Social Policy Approach in a
Godless and Amoral Society
Writings on Philosophy and Economy of Power Vol. 2

ISBN/EAN: 978-3-86741-770-9
First published in 2012 by Europaeischer Hochschulverlag GmbH &
Co KG, Bremen, Germany.

EHV)

Encouraging the stranger in us

Table of Contents

Acknowledgements

My special gratitude goes to the Cairns Institute at the James Cook University. Having been granted a fellowship allowed me to work on completing this project – a book bringing together edited conference papers and presentations. "Editing" means in some cases as well to enhance some ideas that had not been in this way part of the original presentations.

Of course, I want to extend my Thanks to those who made it possible for me to give the original presentations, in particular Gaby Floesser from the local organising committee of the Federal Congress of Social Work in Dortmund; Juhani Laurinkari from the local organising committee for the conference of the The National Social Policy Association in Finland, and Ariane Rodert, Ludvig Sandberg and Goeran Pettersson from the NGO-Forum in Sweden and also Mairéad Considine and Fiona Dukelow from the School of Applied Social Studies, and Peter Kennedy and David O'Connell, Vice President for Research and from his office respectively at the University College of Cork.

Opportunities of taking part and contributing to such events are in many cases more about entering exciting discussions, gaining insight into stimulating ideas and also friendly relationships – not always which makes me even more grateful when I make this experience. Particular Thank You here to Juho Saari, Pauli Niemelae, Veli-Matti Poutanen and surely another time Ariane Rodert, Ludvig Sandberg and Goeran Pettersson.

On the topic running through all the present contributions, I could develop interesting and also very friendly contacts to the Max-Planck Institute for Foreign and International Social Law, Munich, there Ulrich Becker and in particular Hans-F. Zacher. Finally I want to thank Silvia Staub-Bernasconi for the many inspiring talks – be it on the occasion of conferences or in the garden, overlooking Zurich.

It may be symptomatic that special appreciation grew for the engagements with people from outside though there are even two presentations from Cork included – the special appreciation to people and institutions far a field may be symptomatic and if so, it may remain a riddle forever if it is the case because the prophet doesn't count in the own country or because it is on the ground of the freedom gained by striking roots.

Those who read Georg Simmel, know that, importantly, the stranger remains just this: a Stranger.

Peter Herrmann

Science – Social Science – Practice
Or: Searching for Responsibility

Prepared as Part of a Preparation of the Contribution to the UCC Research Highlights Lecture Series at University College of Cork, Ireland; October 2009

Nullum magnum ingenium sine mixtura dementiae fuit.

Seneca

Abstract

Science, if taken the term from its etymological origin, has one engaged leg and one kicking leg. The first is a matter of knowledge, from the Latin scire – knowing and scindere – separate; the second is the reality and practice that is directed towards such reality. All this seems to be very simple as long as we allow ourselves to approach this as a simple and one-dimensional relationship. Such approach is paradoxically based on the wrong assumption of a fundamental split of science and social science and moreover on a division between disciplines. However, this overlooks the generic unity of science which is based in social and societal processes that are concerned with building of property and the emergence of power. And from here another seeming paradox arises: Science that supports proprietors and maintains power, easily undermines the stance for responsible action.

The question – a general one, directed to research as for instance undertaken in the framework of the PRSI-programs as presented in the lecture series last year and not least as question that should be considered for teaching and learning then is: How can we determine the ethics and responsibility of science in today's glocalised world?

In Advance

It is a special honour for me giving this talk: Science – Social Science – Practice is the title and the subtitle reads Searching for Responsibility. It is a topic that is currently en vogue. Richard Sennett published not too long ago a book on the Culture of New Capitalism – or had it been the new Culture of Capitalism? Samir Amin looks at processes of the civilisation of capitalism (see Amin, 2008). José Manuel Barroso, recently approaching his second term in office as president of the European Commission, highlighted in a statement geared to the election that

2

[a]n effective and responsible reform of financial markets must be
implemented swiftly, so as to re-centre markets on the ethical basis
essential for both success and legitimacy.

(Barroso, 2009)

And not least we are in the hands of the claimed universe, Benedict XVIth providing the answer on any question: caritas in veritate.

And actually the pope looks for an answer on the burning questions of our societies: the economy obviously failed – and it failed on grounds of given economic structures.

> *in the pursuit of development, there is a need for "the deep thought and*
> *reflection of wise men in search of a new humanism which will enable*
> *modern man to find himself anew" [Paul VI, Encyclical Letter*
> *Populorum Progressio, 20: loc. cit., 267]. But that is not all.*
> *Underdevelopment has an even more important cause than lack of deep*
> *thought: it is "the lack of brotherhood among individuals and*
> *peoples"[Ibid., 66: loc. cit., 289-290].*

(Benedict XVI, 2009: 27)

This statement is actually made with reference to the encyclical letter Populorum Progressio by Paul VI (from 1967).

Looking at burning issues, indeed; and facing the problems of a seemingly nebulous field – a matter of concealing and conciliation. This leaves us, of course, in a closed room of statements of belief. They may be religious or not – in any case the clear mind is muffled by burning incense.

However, it is seemingly also a very difficult topic: we are in urgent need of answers on most pressing questions: of course first and foremost the global economic crisis, but not less the ongoing devastation of the natural environment, the crisis of the EU which is not at all solved by the results of the referendum but at best confirmed, the crisis of Third-Level Education which may be more visible, but not more real by the financial conditions and the many confirmations of what can be seen as moral decline: officials using helicopters for private trips on account of tax payers, and preaching water to the public – and we are gathering here to talk about very general questions – questions that are employing us for a long time, and repeatedly – we find them in the works of ancient Greek and Roman philosophers. But it is exactly there where we find them as well as imminent practical matters – most pronouncedly and well remembered until today in form of the Hippocratic oath.

Making such reference, we see, however, that the search for responsibility is actually very much about Science, Social Science and Practice – much less than it may appear in the beginning.

But it is an issue which is en vogue as well amongst social scientists which you may consider as representatives of exact social science: economists as Paul Krugman state:

> *Few economists saw our current crisis coming, but this predictive failure was the least of the field's problems. More important was the profession's blindness to the very possibility of catastrophic failures in a market economy.*

> *(Krugman, Paul, 2009)*

And he said that

> *the economics profession went astray because economists, as a group, mistook beauty, clad in impressive-looking mathematics, for truth ... economists fell back in love with the old, idealized vision of an economy in which rational individuals interact in perfect markets, this time gussied up with fancy equations ...*

> *Unfortunately, this romanticized and sanitized vision of the economy led most economists to ignore all the things that can go wrong. They turned a blind eye to the limitations of human rationality that often lead to bubbles and busts; to the problems of institutions that run amok; to the imperfections of markets - especially financial markets - that can cause the economy's operating system to undergo sudden, unpredictable crashes; and to the dangers created when regulators don't believe in regulation.*

> *(ibid.)*

His overall conclusion is then

> *When it comes to the all-too-human problem of recessions and depressions, economists need to abandon the neat but wrong solution of assuming that everyone is rational and markets work perfectly.*

> *(ibid.)*

And actually I received an invitation for a meeting today in Dublin, Joseph Stiglitz talking during a session launching the NESC – Social Report for Ireland on Well-being Matters.

The background of this lecture is the PRTLI – Programme for Research in Third-Level Institutions, aiming on (or claiming) the Irish Research Landscape.

And the background is a division we usually take for granted: the division between science and social science. I mentioned economics seemingly in the middle, on a borderline.

The perspective taken is not an attempt to give final answers – rather I want to put forward some explicitly provocative theses and point on some dilemmas.

SCIENCE   SOCIAL SCIENCE

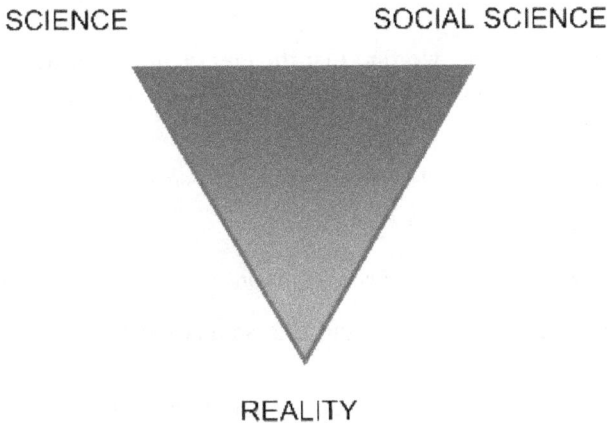

REALITY

Illustration 1

First, even today the division between science and social science is not real and it is only one on the surface though there strongly reinforced. The underlying division is one between scientific exploration and reality. Science today – and by today I do not mean the 21st century but modern science, science as it evolved since, lets say, the Renaissance – acts by and large as 'independent of reality'.

Second – and this is a major paradox – this is a consequence of men gaining the consciousness or at least the feeling of being able to 'replace the Creator'. I am sure that those who know me and I hope that those who don't – will be surprised, hearing me pointing on the problematique of humankind developing skills and the notion of replacing god and making and shaping the world: in science and in social science.

5

Third, the reason behind this is that – this as another provocation – 'god had a plan' whereas humankind had been obsessed by competition, had been fighting over the plan, forced to different competing plans and also loosing the plan out of sight. In other words: the loss of universality, i.e. universal practice led to claims of universality.[1]

Forth, being now seemingly able to create and shape the world humankind gained time – look at the mortality age, look at the fresh strawberries you may enjoy as part of your Christmas dinner and look at the speeding up of flows: communication, travel, data processing etc. But the downside followed on the foot: the loss of time: the acceleration meaning not least the emergence of an overwhelming power of new orders.

So, at the end of all this we find that the emergent complexity means the emergence of a paradox itself – in the words of one of my teachers – Niklas Luhmann:

> *Alles könnte anders sein - und fast nichts kann ich ändern.*
>
> *(Luhmann, 1969: 44)*
>
> *– All could be different but I nearly cannot change anything.*

And it will be later shown: behind this stands the loss of rationality or better the reduction of rationality.

It is from here that I can come back to the beginning, to the first point, the fact that the division we are facing in academia is not the division between science and social science: the underlying division is one between scientific exploration and reality.

So, what is at stance can be put under five broad headings:

- Science and Space
- "The Loss of God"
- The Loss of a Plan
- The Loss of Time

---

[1] Sure, this does not contradict what Marx says in the beginning of Part 3 of the first volume of the Capital, looking at labour: highlighting that it is actually the plan of the product, existing ex ante in the imagination of producer 'stamps it as exclusively human'.; nor does it mean that universal practice had been truly universal – it had been so only in terms of being concerned with and acting with respect of the entirety of the known world.

6

- The Reduction of Rationality

Smart Socio-Economies

So, if it is about space, let us have a look at space:

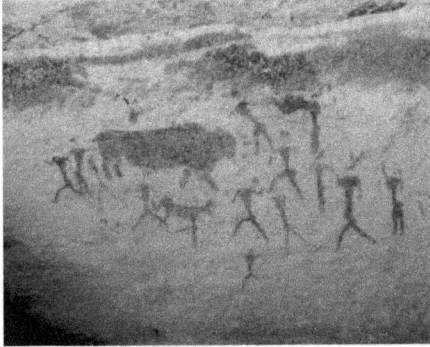

Illustration 2[2]

Here we see an early smart society, a smart economy: It had been smart by being a social economy in the sense of an entity. It had been a smart social economy by power as entity of ability, mastery and command – command over nature and over people. We can characterise this kind of society as well by the integrity of four factors: the complexity of the system, corresponding with the power to change – or maintain – things according to a known, assessable direction of change and a high degree of social integrity.

Excursus: The Double-Character of Power

We should briefly sojourn on this topic: power – as it is a central topic of the further considerations. Of course, centrality applies on the one hand by way of our societies being figurations that are based on inequality of power: a matter of access, control and – open or subtle suppression, going hand in hand with patterns of general inequality. Such general inequality is a matter of both, control over own, personal circumstances and also inequality over social conditions and developments, be they of immediate relevance as matter of living conditions or be it as matter of control over the secular development of society as such. Though the

---

[2] http://www.willgoto.com/images/Size3/South_Africa_KwaZulu_Natal_Bush man_Painting_26d16a38842a4787a965a9cec1397465.jpg; 10.08.2012

latter may sound at first glance very abstract it is an issue that surely is much more concrete than we may assume. Consider the frequent statements by so many 'ordinary people' who accept certain hardship, wishing that 'my children will hopefully be better off one day in their own life.' There is surely much that can be said on this – but at least one thing that surely stands in one or another form behind such statement is that people strive – in their own way, in the way that reflects their own horizon of experiences, recognised and perceived experience etc. with respect to time and space – to shape society.[3] The point I want to address here – and which will frequently come up again – is the double nature of power which is frequently overlooked – and which equally frequently leads and leaves us to a condemnation of power –going however hand in hand with a clandestine admiration.

Looking at power in its original meaning we see that it is addressing an issue which is, though surely linked to control – very much a matter of the constitution of mutual relationships. Building such relationship had been based on two principal orientations: the one is the concern with appropriation: establishing a relationship between humans and their environment, i.e. the search for the answer of the question: how can I/we accommodate ourselves in the socio-natural environment. The other aspect is already said with this formulation and it consists on two points. (i) it is about the fact that the natural environment is considered as socio-natural matter and (ii) it is about accommodation in this environment. In other words, we are first and foremost concerned with a modus that is not striving for a simple subordination of nature under human needs – accommodation goes beyond that and includes some kind of mutual respect. This does not claim that this relationship was not exploitative – nomadism showed very much that the contrary had been the case. The seeming "replacability" of a given environment by moving to another space allowed the ruthless exploitation. However, saying that the relationship can be seen as 'accommodation' means that the human being did not distance itself from the rest of nature but saw him/herself very much as part of it and with this also recognised itself as in different ways depending on it – rather than being able to establish a relationship of subordination. As such it meant strife, it meant respect and it meant the search for meaning in a very specific – and perhaps peculiar sense, peculiar as it presupposes a contradiction between the actor and an object

---

[3] Here it t can remain open if or if not this is just a pattern that follows the mode of individualist rationalism or if this is socially oriented behaviour – and in which way these different layers are interwoven and/or contradicting each other.

or at least a fundamental separation between the two: the meaning had to be derived from defining the own power in terms of abilities –in English language we use still the term of 'having power over' also as way of describing the ability to manage a certain task although it is not really meant to deal with any simple ability but only with the ability of doing something very specific, namely something that requires the control over something or somebody. Against this we may turn to the interpretation of a postmodern interpretation of power given by Frank C. Richardson's and Robert C. Bishop's who say that

> [t]urning to the postmodern or poststructuralist take on power, Foucault (1980), for example, sharply criticizes conventional modern liberal notions of power that describe its effects mainly in 'negative' terms as something that 'excludes,' 'dominates,' 'represses,' or 'censors.' Rather, he speaks of 'relations of power' that in a more 'positive' sense produce forms of life and also fields of knowledge, including all of their possible statements about what is true or false, good or evil. Power is not something that is 'possessed' but rather is 'exercised'.

> (Richardson/Bishop, 2004: 189 f.)

The crucial point is to develop an understanding of the complexity of power. On the one hand this has to recognise the positive potential of power as moment of formation and transformation of socio-environmental processes on the basis of rationality. On the other hand it has to recognise also the 'competitive' dimension of power that arises from and perpetuates inequality – be it based on brute force and coercion or on complex patterns of hegemonic manipulations. Importantly we have to recognise that in this light the term empowerment may indicate a change or it may also well indicate a problematic stance of such concepts that – though perhaps unknowingly and with without wanting to do so – puts people in competitive perspectives. A major problem arising from this consideration is that in contemporary societies empowerment has indeed always to consider as well the hegemonic patterns. Empowerment will – perhaps leaving some exceptional situations aside – always have to deal with power being a 'contested good'. Moreover, this can only be understood if it is conceptualised by establishing a link to property – though property itself has to be understood as complex issue with the two dimension of possession – as matter of legal ownership – and appropriation – as matter of control in its actual dimension of soci(et)al practice *(see for further reflections on this as well Herrmann, Peter, forthcoming b)*.

Importantly, some recent shifts of re-personalisation of power are not least at the same time very much also a matter of increasing 're-socialisation'. This is at least true in the sense of the direct control being regained by individuals and 'their networks'. Corporate dominance in policy processes has this side in the same way as we can see these patterns in some political movements on the left that, though not being communitarian,[4] emphasise the close link between personality (which frequently emerges to a charismatic figure) and basis democratic structures or 'un-structures'.

Of course, in one or another way, the entire process of relating to the environment – not least as it had been understood in its socio-natural character – had been also very much a matter of incorporating other people and relating to other people into this relationship. And at this point we find the – in the beginning a potential, later a real – shift in the meaning of power. What begins as power as matter of abilities to accommodate oneself in and as part of nature emerges as matter of accommodating oneself in a social relationship of dealing together, in mutual action with nature and shifts from there towards a third stage, namely 'sorting', i.e. organising and managing the relationship between the different actors themselves. The important point is that we now enter a new historical era: that from a Trinitarian worldview towards a Quatritarian perspective – this is shown, of course only with a very broad brush, in the following.

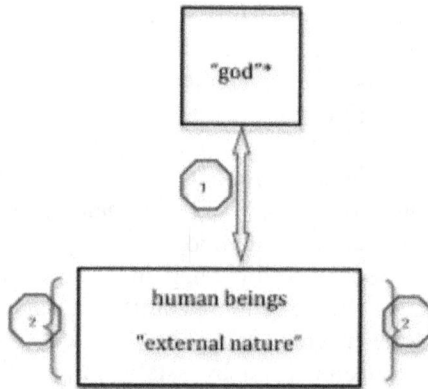

Figure 1

---

* 'God' is not been meant in the strict sense but refers to any wider belief system, capturing something 'unexplained' and being seen as inexplicable – or at most to be explained by making reference to some kind of external force.

Relation ➋ is characterised by the fact that it is located in the immediacy of the togetherness and even identity of the relevant forces.

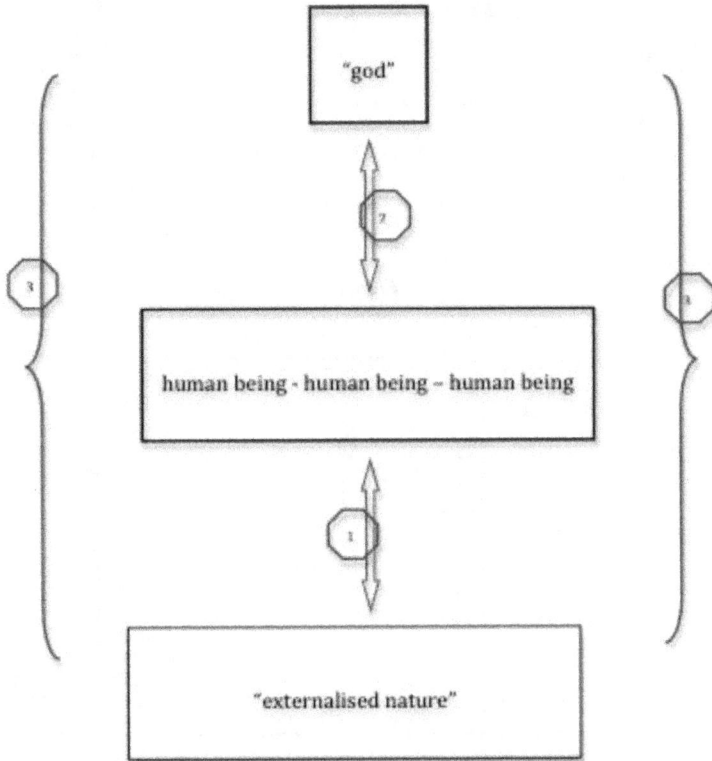

Figure 2

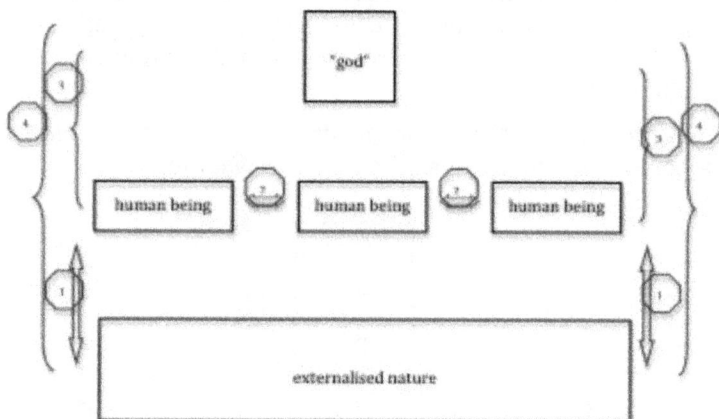

Figure 3

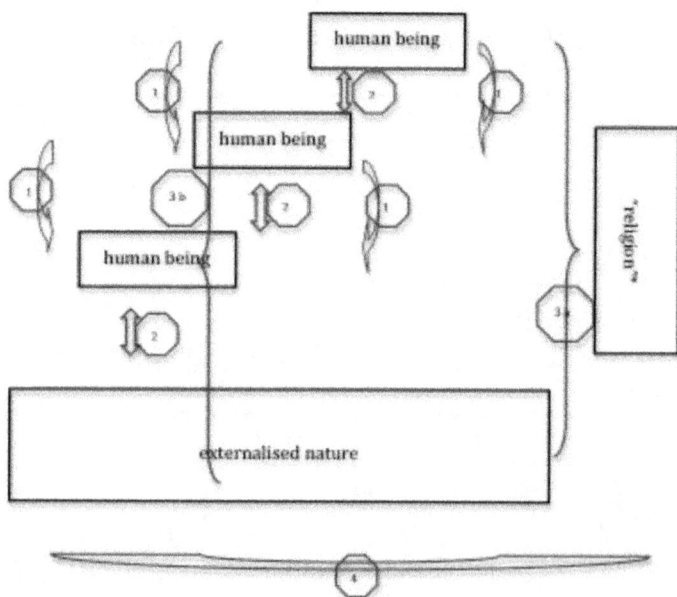

Figure 4

* Here we speak of 'religion' rather than 'god'. As already mentioned, 'god' had not been meant in the strict sense nit referred to any wider belief system capturing something 'unexplained' and being seen as inexplicable – or at most to be explained by making reference to some kind of external force. Religious here refers to the same basic principle but is now linked to a strictly institutionalised system.

This is linked with the **relation ③ a;** other relations – abstract or concrete "reference to ideas, beliefs, systems of thought, worldviews etc. that are meant to give an overall coherence, i.e. provide a perspective on the universe, would now be captured by the reference to **relation ③ b.**

With respect to **relation ②** it is important to note that this is we are here dealing with the relationship between humans and nature. However, such relationship can be immediate or mediated – by tools, machinery or social organisation/management. The kind of dominant relationship of not only one between individuals/social groups but also one that is tightly intermingled with (being based on and basis for) domination of specific distribution of economic sectors (primary, secondary, tertiary) and from here with certain stages of the development productive forces, and modes of production and (subsequently) accumulation regimes, reflecting secular developments *(see in this context Herrmann, Peter forthcoming a – with reference to Marx' Grundrisse the process of differentiation is elaborated by looking at the development from an integrated understanding of production as all-encompassing process to an understanding of production – consumption – distribution – exchange as separate spheres, and later moreover as spheres of which the 'latter comes first, and the entire process and structure being turned on its head'. This is on the one hand understood as secular process reflecting such change of the productive forces as matter of socialisation As such it is also very much a matter of changes in the re-distribution of positions within the world system and countries lagging behind in technical and 'terms of capitalist welfare' and their relative success in catching up.*[5] *On the other hand this reflects in the concrete occurrence and pattern as well specific cyclical amplitudes, then being specifically linked to cyclical crisis, for instance in form of over-accumulation patterns).*

---

[5] This 'success' has to be seen as matter of pull and push effects – countries are drawn more closely and directly into capitalist process of capitalist valorisation. And this opens for them opportunities to exploit their 'relative advantages' as for instance the processing of available raw materials, cheap labour, specific socio-demographic patterns as the prevalence of family business structures and the like.

Relation ④ is emerging from the new position of religion (or 'god' respectively) – on this stage it is 'sidelined' rather than featuring simply as superimposed and absolute entity in a hierarchical system. But the sidelining is not only an issue due to general trends towards secularisation as they are looked at throughout the remainder of this contribution but also an issue of an emerging competition between different religions – now as institutionalised system –, religion and other faith-based systems and these systems and other systems that have or claim universalist and universalising explanatory character of ..., well the universe. It is the interplay of the tendency of secularisation and emerging competition that makes such process of horizontal relation so important. A crucial point is in this context that in this way on the one hand on the one hand hegemony of one system can be maintained and at the same time some kind of 'pluralism' can be fostered within this hegemonic system.

What may appear at first glance as dispersal of power is in actual fact not more than a different form of power execution – more subtle as now meant to be power of socialisation; and also more direct as it is now dealing with inequalities within the system *(the dominant **relations** ⑦)* rather than the difference between systems.

Coming then from here back to power in a perspective of differentiation, we can say that an entity, with an 'overriding point'[6] of 'the unexplained' shifted towards a system of inner differentiation by way of internalising the original difference to the external world: the knowledge difference, i.e. the previously unexplained may still remain not being understood. However, on this new stage they are at least defined as a question with which the system, i.e. the living together had to deal with. In other words: they are now seen as challenge that is at least in principle manageable and has to be tackled by humans. And with this, 'nature' got paradoxically increasingly defined as external, different from socialising humanity. In a third step, then, it is not far to go to social differentiation. Linking this into a theory of power we can see the internalisation of an up to then external power differential. But what is far more: the power differential that is up to then more or less entirely defined in technical terms – as matter of the control, or even: the (perceived) controllability – is now redefined and both transformed and translated into a social matter.

This is – in the first instance – not necessarily a matter of principle inequality tat cannot be overcome: on the contrary, in the first instance

---

[6]   'overriding' not primarily in a hierarchical sense

the internalisation of power can be seen as systematic approach of constituting the social. Referring to the work of the European Foundation of Social Quality we understand the social as the outcome of the interaction between people (constituted as actors) and their constructed and natural environment. With this in mind its subject matter refers to people's productive and reproductive relationships. In other words

- the constitutive interdependency between processes of self-realisation and processes of the formation of collective identities
- is a condition for 'the social', realised by the interactions of
  - o actors, being – with their self-referential capacity – competent to act
  - o and their framing structure, which translates immediately into the context of human relationships.

Bringing this together with what had been established by the graphs, we can clearly see the present perspective on power. In the first instance we had been looking at power as matter of establishing a firm position in the real world. Social relationships at this stage can be very much seen as spontaneously developing alongside, being matters of an integrated relationship between humans and nature. With the historical development, however, the social dimension gains its own value as matter of a consciously and systematically controlled and even designed moment – still tightly knit into the way of dealing with the relationship between humans and nature. However, parallel to the primitive accumulation of capital we find a turn in the power relationship *(illustrated in* Figure 3, *page 12):* Decisive is not the partial separation between human and nature, but the clear distinction between humans, going beyond mechanisms of 'organisational and technical division of labour'. Émile Durkheim's statement is important here, making explicit that

> *[t]he division of labor is not peculiar to the economic world; we can observe its growing influence in the most varied fields for society. The political, administrative, and judicial functions are growing more and more specialized. It is the same with the aesthetic and scientific functions.*

> *(Durkheim, 1893: 40)*

and concluding that

> *[s]uch fact cannot be produced without profoundly affecting our moral constitution; for the development of man will be conceived in two entirely different ways, depending on whether we yield to the movement or resist it.*
>
> *(ibid.:41)*

This is most important in the light of Durkheim's notion to see this as secular process of which

> *it can even be said that the more specialized the functions of the organism, the greater its development.*
>
> *(ibid.)*

Of course, already this short exploration shows two major problems with Émile Durkheim's approach. First, it remains unclear in its definition – sharing blurring borders with fragmentation, specialisation, co-operation.[7] Second, the more serious problem is that Durkheim sees it as part of a secular movement, linking it as such to a specific understanding of 'progress' and allowing John Arundel Barnes to say that

> *Durkheim admits as division of labour only those kinds of occupational specialisation which satisfy the relationship between division of labour and social solidarity that he is seeking to demonstrate.*
>
> *(Barnes, J.A., 1966: 165)*

Karl Marx, on the other hand, emphasises the underlying economic mechanism, but goes much beyond traditional understandings in mainstream economics. The main point in question of a difference is that we are now not taking individual's behaviour as point of departure but two major social dimensions. (i) power and (ii) accumulation.

As well known, the normal approach to division of labour refers by and large to the classical understanding which poses on the utilitarian assumption the simple desire improve individual happiness – and we can justifiably leave it open what happiness actually means, be it a matter of enhancing the availability of material resources/utility goods or the way of 'easing' ways of dealing with something or something or other things. An important point of departure is already Bernard Mandeville's exploration

---

[7]   for instance mentioned when he looks at law; ibid.: 122 ff.

16

Man, as I have hinted before, naturally loves to imitate what he sees others do, which is the reason that savage people all do the same thing: this hinders them from meliorating their condition, though they are always wishing for it: but if one will wholly apply himself to the making of bows and arrows, whilst another provides food, a third build huts, a fourth makes garments, and a fifth utensils: they not only become useful to one another, but the callings and employments themselves will in the same number of years receive much greater improvements, than if all would have been promiscuously followed by every one of the five.

(Mandeville, 1714: 465)

This had been further explored in the utilitarian spirit in particular by Francis Hutcheson in his look at *A System of Moral Philosophy* highlighting that

'tis plain that a man in absolute solitude tho' he were of mature strength, and fully instructed in all our arts of life, could scarcely procure to himself the bare necessaries of life, even in the best foils or climates; much less could he procure any grateful conveniences.

(Hutcheson, 1755: 287 f.)

However, as much as this takes a social dimension for granted, it is doing this only to the extent of individuals (i) pooling resources and – perhaps more importantly – (ii) doing so on the basis of calculating opportunity costs. It is in this context notable that Hutcheson and also Adam Smith strongly orient on the role of the division of labour as means of increasing the output of production. So we read in the *Wealth of Nations* of three aspects of increasing productivity by division of labour.

First, the improvement of the dexterity of the workman necessarily increases the quantity of the work he can perform; and the division of labour, by reducing every man's business to some simple operation, and by making this operation the sole employment of his life, necessarily increases very much the dexterity of the workman.

(Smith, 1776: 7)

He continues after a brief explanation:

Secondly, the advantage which is gained by saving the time commonly lost in passing from one sort of work to another is much greater than we should at first view be apt to imagine it.

(ibid.: 8)

A further point remains to be pointed out:

> *Thirdly, and lastly, everybody must be sensible how much labour is facilitated and abridged by the application of proper machinery. It is unnecessary to give any example. I shall only observe, therefore, that the invention of all those machines by which labour is so much facilitated and abridged seems to have been originally owing to the division of labour.*
>
> *(ibid.: 9; cf. Hutcheson, op.cit.: 288 f.)*

With this both, Smith and Hutcheson see also private property legitimised and the ground for accumulation provided, Frances Hutcheson saying

> *Depriving any Person of the Fruits of his own innocent Labour. Takes away all Motives to Industry from Self-Love; or the nearer Ties; and leaves us no other Motive than general Benevolence: nay, it exposes the Industrious as a constant Prey to the Slothful, and sets Self-Love against Industry. This is the right Ground of our Right of Dominion and Property in the Fruits of our Labours.*
>
> *(Hutcheson, 1738[4]: 285)*

And continuing then by unfolding

> *Industry will be confin'd to our present Necessities, and cease when they are provided for; at least it will only continue from the weak Motive of general Benevolence, if we are not allow'd to store up beyond present Necessity, and to dispose of what is above our Necessities, either in Barter for other kinds of Necessarys, or for the Service of our Friends or Familys.*
>
> *(ibid., 286)*

Two further points are important:

(i) Having said that this process runs parallel to the primitive accumulation, does not suggest that we are solely dealing with a mechanical political replication of the economic process in the political realm. Initially such interpretation of stating such separation would actually not make much sense to the extent to which the two areas are build an entity and we can actually find a foundation of power not in a strict economic sphere but we see a quite independent political process to the extent as the separation between economy and politics is not fully in place *(see on this tentative remarks in Herrmann, 2010 (b)).*[8] However, we find this separation as definite overcoming of preceding triangularism: rather than being concerned with the three relational questions, put forward in Figure 2 *on page 11* – ① between humans and nature, ② humans and 'god' and ③ the overall relationship of the universe – we are now *(*Figure 3*, page 12)* concerned with a quatritarian pattern – the relationship between ① humanity and externalised nature, ② amongst humans, ③ humanity and 'god', and finally ④ again the 'universe'. It is only on the basis of this twofold separation – or externalisation – possible that the meaning of power moves away from its original meaning, being increasingly concerned with the regulation of the newly developing internalities, i.e. the relationship amongst humans. The external matters – nature and 'god' alike – are gaining more and more an instrumental character (appropriation of nature as means of underpinning social power positions, in general the question of ruling) and/or a role as intermediaries (religion as means of political steering and governing, in general the question of establishing hegemony). This is necessary condition for emergence of ruling and hegemony though not ample condition. It is the first step for the later fundamental shift of the meaning of power: after a time of the original – technical – concern swirling around the new – social – meaning, being finally turned into a relationship that is principally defined as political matter, concerned with regulating inequality of access to the resources and the (access to) means of production. The emergence of economy as differentiated system stands as midwife at the crèche of a new era: an era that is characterised by the paradox of politics gaining the fundamentally distinct role of a means of ruling, a means of dealing now with hierarchies rather than cooperation.

(ii) How does this link to the system-theoretical perspective of differentiation? To recap, such perspective refers by and large to three different modes of differentiation, namely segmentary, social and functional differentiation *(see Luhmann, 1990; Luhmann, 1982)*. One of the main problems with such perspective is that it does not reflect on power as basic constitutional principle of existence. One could go even a step further by saying that systems-theory is in some fundamental respect

---

[8] Of course, this is a difficult topic and various different positions are taken. The statement here does not claim a real independence of the political sphere. Probably the easiest way to present this is by highlighting the dependence of political power on material resources, however not following mechanisms of economic processes in the strict sense.

geared towards harmonisation, (1) fading power questions out by interpreting them at most towards the relationship between different systems – it will then be easily translated into economic terminology and suggested to be a matter of the externalisation of costs – and/or (2) re-interpreting them as technicality – here it is easy to translate the issues in question as matters of 'neutral and inherent practical constraint', or as 'political technology' to borrow a term from Michel Foucault – and with the same author we can go further and see it as part of

> *the way by which, through some political technology of individuals, we have been led to recognize ourselves as a society, as part of a social entity, as part of a nation or of a state.*

> *(Foucault, 1988: 145)*

In consequence, a system-theoretical stance is not in a position to elaborate the most important issue of power as in terms of the reality of its twofold meanings. It is a perfectly suitable tool[9] in order to understand the mechanisms of the inherent workability of the systems themselves. As such it pertains what Michel Foucault highlights as answer on the question for the 'reason of the state' – and cum grano salis this is the general pattern systems-theory is easily able to capture and concentrates on. He disquiets that

> *at the time, what people had in mind was a rationality specific to the art of governing states. From where does this specific art of government draw its rationale? The answer to this question, provoked at the beginning of the seventeenth century, is the scandal of the nascent political thought, and yet the answer, following the authors I have quoted,[10] was very simple. The art of governing people is rational on the condition that it observes the nature of what is governed, that is, the state itself.*

> *(ibid: 149)*

Cum grano salis, the same pattern is widely applied also in contemporary social research, for instance in social reporting, reflecting very much the pattern Foucault mentions and also pertaining it in 'concrete policy design' *(the same happens also in the practice of 'civil society' development, see in addition to the still interesting study by Robert Michels [Michels, 1915], as just one more recent case study of many:*

---

[9] 'Perfectly suitable tool' does by no means suggest that it is the only tool tough.
[10] He refers to Botero, Palazzo, Chemnitz

Pauline Jones Luong and Erika Weinthal [Jones Luong, Pauline/Weinthal, Erika, 1999]; for some general and theoretical reflections on EUropean developments: Herrmann, 2006). Raymond Apthorpe brings up this painful subject when looking at human development reporting, introducing a socio-anthropological perspective. Stating that

> *no distinction is made between what we may call 'reasons of government' and 'reasons of development', which are of course far from being the same in poor countries as in rich*

> *(Apthorpe, 1997: 25),*

he makes us aware of the same factor as mentioned by Foucault, and then challenges the mainstream by asking for

> *researched development reports which go into complexities of links between ideological, institutional, organisational and actual practice, as well as seeing the point of making such distinctions about 'the market' (and other key words).*

> *(ibid.: 26)*

Against this background Apthorpe reiterates some more general problems on the methodological level, namely the challenge to unseal the relationship between the specific-concrete, the general-concrete, the specific-general and the general-abstract. He addresses this by looking at structuralism, pointing out that

> *one of the comparative advantages of received 'structuralism' in social anthropology is that it can treat what it portrays as cultural universals cognitively, as making up 'elementary' and other logical systems. Because these systems are conceptualised aprioristically, they can with truth be said to be imposed when they are found. Thus structural anthropology does, and must, work in a highly abstract and formalist language*

> *(ibid.: 30).*

However, an in such way limited approach fundamentally underscores the individualist approach, ontologically underlying the emerging understanding of power and overcoming power imbalances. It allows only for looking at what Brent D. Slife presents as weak form of relationality, i.e.

[r]elationships and practices [that] are reciprocal exchanges of
information among essentially self-contained organisms, ...
[remaining] ultimately a type of individualism or atomism.

(Slife, 2004: 158)

Coming back to systems-theory, it fundamentally fails when it comes to the question of operations on the wider level – the only offer is, then, the externalisation. This surely is one – and actually a very important – mechanisms of systems to deal with conflicts. However, it remains insufficient in providing a perspective on a more fundamental character of relationships, i.e. strong relationality. Referring another time to Slife we can provide the following understanding:

Strong relationality, by contrast, is an ontological relationality.
Relationships are not just the interactions of what was originally non
relational; relationships are relational 'all the way down.' Things are
not first self-contained entities and then interactive. Each thing,
including each person, is first and always a nexus of relations.

(ibid.: 159)

(i) By introducing such ontological shift into consideration we see already a problem on the surface level. Systems-theory is barely able to contribute to addressing questions dealing with (principal) systemic conflicts.

This brings us back to the question of the primitive accumulation – and from this perspective, still far from being concerned with replication, we are very close to discussing the genuine shift that characterises the process.

Explanations of this process are in many cases based on the idea of division of labour as decisive moments. The principal dividing line in explaining this developmental step goes by seeing it on the one hand as process that is approached on the basis of methodological individualism and rational choice (both taken in a wide understanding). It is individual rationality that makes some individuals perform better than others – this does not need further exploration here and the brief remark which had been already made by quoting Francis Hutcheson will do suffice *(see 18)*.

At least we could see already from there that the primitive accumulation is very much interpreted a 'technical matter': (i) specialisation and concentration of capabilities are seen at the outset, allowing higher productivity; (ii) leading in combination with frugality und vigilance when making use of the gains of production to the occurrence of the initial advantage that allows developing further accumulation.

Paradoxically, it is in this case that the bourgeois economics takes an at least seemingly materialist point of departure, taking economic behaviour as reference. However, this is only at first glance the case as the reference is behaviour rather than the economic constellation – and its development according to a universal regularity – as such. And it is 'rational *individual* behaviour' rather than the social configuration.

With this in mind, we can re-approach the matter and arrive at a different approach. The historical analysis shows – this had been already mentioned – that we do not find an initial separation of politics and economics. Rather, the original constellation is lead by an economy that is characterised by (i) the process of production as complex entity. This means that the formation had been based on two main notions: the one is that of subsistence economy – we can see this as an 'internal' reference: the producer and the immediate entity that is involved in 'production' and 'consumption'. Division of labour exists, though being marginal. It has technical but also social dimensions to it. The latter means that there are as well some exclusionary mechanisms already in force. The other notion is – externally oriented and dealing with certain productive surplus – very much a barter economy. Thus, surplus value, if we may use that term, is not based in the productive process as such, i.e. we are not dealing with surplus value in the strict sense. Instead, it is additional, i.e. redundant produce, exceeding from good management, exceptional conditions and exchange. So, one may say: it is actually not "economically produced" surplus value.

(ii) This is important not only for the functioning as matter of continuous reproduction but furthermore also – and even more – the decisive moment when it comes to development – broadly understood as matter of reproduction on an extended scale. Production of redundant or surplus value is already on this stage more a matter of developing and executing power that is not a matter inherent in economic immediacy. Rather, the relationship is turned around: whereas production in the strict sense is still very much a matter of generating value in the productive sphere and moreover as matter of producing utility value. And this is decisive: we are not yet dealing with the production of exchange value in its own terms and rights. Taking a metaphor, we may say that in consequence the exchange value has to be levered out of the productive sphere in order to be available outside: transformed into a tradable good. It is a twofold process though appearing as political-economic entity: it is – on this stage – indeed the process of politically redefining what the economic value is. This means that value – by the redefinition of its substance: being first utility value and now exchange value – is shifted from production to exchange; and with this it is shifted in a second step (on the same stage) also in formal terms as matter of redefining the ownership. This transformation is not part of the immediate economic process or of rational behaviour of individuals. Rather it is a matter of political violence, of use of brute power in the first instance – her we can refer not least to the explorations of primitive or original accumulation as explored by Karl Marx.

It has to be manifested again that this primitive accumulation is condition for later accumulation not only and not primarily in terms of allowing the accumulation of a sufficient amount of capital for further accumulation. Rather, at stake is the disentanglement of exchange value from utility value; with this the translation of the division of labour into a socio-economic instance rather than a socio-technical instance; in consequence this means the establishment of two distinct spheres, namely economy and politics (or even economy and society as somewhat separate spheres); and it finally – and only now – allows that force is replaced by a 'new form of power', namely the power of the economic process itself. Power based on availability of resources and execution of force is replaced by the 'power of equality': the exchange of labour against money as formally 'just' process – presented in the words by Karl Marx:

> For the conversion of his money into capital, therefore, the owner of money must meet in the market with the free labourer, free in the double sense, that as a free man he can dispose of his labour-power as his own commodity, and that on the other hand he has no other commodity for sale, is short of everything necessary for the realisation of his labour-power.

(Marx, Karl, 1867: 118)

We can raise from here a thesis for further development – and it had been already tentatively and in other words developed in the previous publication *(see Herrmann, 2010 (b))*: This process of primitive accumulation has historically two dimensions. The one is the very primitive form as matter of the forming of capitalism – as such it had been dealt with by Karl Marx and in different dimensions analysed in the context of research on world systems theory. The second dimension is concerned with a cyclical development in medium and long-term time lines. Here we envisage periods of over-accumulation. Each of these periods means that the process of realisation of capital is confronted with the need to levering new means out of the productive process in the strict sense and transform them into a new area of generating value, namely exchange value. We may also say it is about the inclusion of an increasing number of activities into the realm of the productive sphere – or the sphere that is defined as being productive and/or should be part of the process of accumulation.

The Renaissance had been such a major step, seriously enhancing trade and building up a major block of finance capital, however finding its foundation in a tree revolutionary changes in the productive sphere (revolutionary changes that in several cases had been based on the open application of brute violence). (i) One change had been the simple enhancement of the productive basis by enormous progress in the development of tools, technologies and machines *(see Braudel 1967 et altera; for a broad overview: History, 2010)*. (ii) Another important change – seemingly only on the level of circulation – is the enormous development of logistic, not least as matter of improved navigation. The immediate effects on production had been the expansion of markets on the one hand and the new raw materials (or the increased accessibility which allowed an easier inclusion also into traditional processes of production). (iii) We see with its obvious effect on production also the increased – and structurally changed – availability of cheap work force. This had been not least a matter of the emerging possibility of exploitation of workforce which remained itself outside of the societies in question. And against this background it can also be understood that the eradication of entire, for the time in question huge, estates (as the one which had been 'replaced' for the palace in Florence) had been very much also a matter of externalising workforce: the pauperisation of the emerging working 'class' and also of groups of former craftsmen. – One may add a further aspect – the development of arts: with the shape of 'industrialised production of arts works'[11] and in consequence the dimensions.[12]

---

[11] see the arts industrial workshop of Andrea di Cione [Verrocchio], himself remaining by and large unknown but providing the crèche Leonardo da Vinci, Michelangelo di Lodovico Buonarroti Simoni and Rembrandt Harmenszoon van Rijn, in the latter case especially interesting in connection with the meaning of guilds as regulators of arts production

[12] From the very high end products, institutionally ordered as the exhibits of papal and increasingly secular political and 'consumptive' (by the Nouveau Riche of the time) power alike

With all these different developments, mutually depending on each other and mutually reinforcing – we find a fundamental, not to say: *foundational,* shift of production and also of the entire accumulation regime, mode of regulation and social fabrique. As much as it meant a change of the composition of capital in economic terms, (of which the organic composition of capital is only one, though a central factor), it meant as well a change of the composition of the 'social capital' – Pierre Bourdieu looked at relevant dimensions in his work *(see for instance Bourdieu, 1983; Bourdieu, Pierre, 1986).* And thus it meant not least a fundamental, and again foundational shift of power and power relations.

We can see very similar patterns today with the new developments leading towards establishing hyper-finance capitalism. On the one hand it is already since some time geared towards the inclusion of ever more areas of social and private life into the circle of economic valuation (or shall we better speak of their subordination under these premises?); on the other hand and with this it is the establishment of reflexive mechanisms conjoined with this inclusion/subordination: the capitalisation of capitalisation itself.

Especially as reaction on the recent crisis much ink had been employed to highlight the boundless scope of this process – and also on providing an analysis of the various mechanisms behind these processes. And important discussions also concern ethical issues, personal responsibility and the reach of law to control these processes. In a lecture on the crisis of the finance market capitalism, Joerg Huffschmidt elaborated on some basic economic problems, pointing on especially five points. These are outlined in the following:

- the divergence between finance capital and social product since 1980 – whereas the first multiplied by 16, the latter only by 5.5;

- the international character of the financial assets, i.e. their origin in another country than that of its current location which is a trend that can be found in developed and developing countries alike;

- the permanent redistribution of income from the bottom to the top from which a lack of purchasing power is the unavoidable consequence;

- the tendency to privatise the pension funds with the consequence of huge amounts of capital being held in private finance schemes rather than money being paid to the pensioners in PAYG-schemes;

- the liberalisation of capital movement which means that investment can be undertaken in any place which had been limited under the Bretton Woods system.

(see Huffschmid, 2009)

According to Huffschmid, these factors can explain to a large extent the foundation and emergence of the finance market capitalism, being established on the fact that now owners of finance capital are looking for investment opportunity whereas in industrial capitalism the capitalist who wanted to invest into productive processes looked for capital that would allow him doing this.[13]

John Bellamy Foster and Robert W. McChesney, in a remarkably comprehensive article highlight the basic socio-economic features of Monopoly-Finance Capital and the Paradox of Accumulation by pointing on the

> *'stagnation-financialisation trap', whereby financial expansion has become the main 'fix' for the system, yet is incapable of overcoming the underlying structural weakness of the economy. Much like drug addiction, new, larger fixes are required at each point merely to keep the system going.*

> *(Foster/McChesney, 2009)*

This is a matter that will be employed on a later occasion but that is important already in the present context in general terms and that gains especial importance as it allows us considering various issues on the emergence of *New Princedoms (Herrmann, 2010 (b))* more in depth. Probably more remarkable is that very similar debates can be found much earlier. In an essay in the Monthly review, titled *Financial Instability: Where will it all End?,* Harry Magdoff and Paul M. Sweezy noted importantly that the financial crisis of the time had been only a reflection of the actual crisis, namely the disfunctioning productive

---

[13] A few short contributions on the crisis may be named – though in a way randomly chosen, they are mentioned (i) to show the variety of interpretations and (ii) underlining that in one way or another we are not dealing with 'automatic processes', emerging from isolated economic developments that take place 'without actors' but with processes that are made by human actors: classes and individuals alike: *Zinn, 2010 a, b; Grinin/Korotayev, 2010, especially also highlighting the possible positive effects of finance markets, comparing it with the meaning of railway in previous times; Rügemer, 2010*

system *(see Magdoff/Sweezy, 1982)*. And they conclude with a quote taken from a column in the New York Times, written by Karen Lissakers:

> *Citibank's Walter Wriston said in 1979, "Whether we like it or not, mankind now has a completely integrated, international financial and informational marketplace capable of moving money and ideas to any place on this planet in minutes." The machine is also capable of stopping. Mr. Wriston and his colleagues—whether they like it or not— need the kind of government regulation and support that prevent abuse of the system when everybody is happy and keep the wheels turning when everyone is sad.*
>
> *(Lissakers, 1982 quoted in: Magdoff/Sweezy, 1982: 4)*

There hadn't been any solution since then – rather, we see an increasing aggrevation and a lengthy quote, taken from Immanuel Wallerstein's *Harold Wolpe Lecture* at the *University of KwaZulu-Natal* may be allowed. He states

> *The difference this time has been the scale of the speculation and the indebtedness. After the biggest A-period expansion in the history of the capitalist world-economy, there has followed the biggest speculative mania. The bubbles moved through the whole world-system -- from the national debts of the Third World countries and the socialist bloc in the 1970s, to the junk bonds of large corporations in the 1980s, to the consumer indebtedness of the 1990s to the U.S. government indebtedness of the Bush era. The system has gone from bubble to bubble. The world is currently trying one last bubble -- the bailouts of the banks and the printing of dollars.*
>
> *The depression into which the world has fallen will continue now for quite a while and go quite deep. It will destroy the last small pillar of relative economic stability, the role of the U.S. dollar as a reserve currency of safeguarding wealth. As this happens, the main concern of every government in the world -- from the United States to China, from France to Russia to Brazil to South Africa, not to speak of all the weaker governments on the world scene -- will be to avert the uprising of the unemployed workers and the middle strata whose savings and pensions disappear. The governments are turning to protectionism and printing money as their first line of defense, as ways of dealing with popular anger.*
>
> *Such measures may postpone the dangers the governments fear and may assuage momentarily the pain of ordinary people. But they will eventually probably make the situation even worse. We are entering a gridlock of the system, from which the world will find it extremely difficult to extract itself. The gridlock will express itself in the form of a constant set of ever wilder fluctuations, which will make short-term*

predictions -- both economic and political -- virtually guesswork. And
this in turn will aggravate the popular fears and alienation.

(Wallerstein, 2009)

In a wider sociological perspective the classification and assessment of the development has to draw attention to the contradictory character of process.

On the one hand we have to acknowledge the real danger of a development to the far right – but not simply in terms of a further development of 'conservative socio-economic policies' and the real danger of even fascist developments. Equally dangerous is the development as it had been outlined on another occasion, captured under the heading of a re-feudalisation and marked by the (re-)subjectivation of power *(see Herrmann, 2010 (b))*.

As important as it is to characterise the process as one of capitalisation (of which commodification is only one consequence), we are in the very same framework also dealing with a process of socialisation. Moreover, and as it is well known, we can interpret capitalisation also as a 'limited way of socialisation'. An example par excellence is housework. As much as we may lament when considering the commercialisation of 'genuine sustenance work' in the households – and bemoan in this context also the breaking away of genuine communication; as much as we have to criticise the commodification of care services and the specific mode of professionalization it takes under these conditions we should never forget that all this nevertheless serves in some ways as liberalising factor especially of the life of many women. It is this very same process that actually replicates the problematique of power: it is actually a shift in the interpretation of the specific social character that is decisive – not the question of privatisation versus socialisation in an apparent way *(i.e. taking Slife's term again: not as weak relationality)* but the question of privatisation as substantial matter *(i.e. as strong relationality)*. And here we finding both cases the same pattern – in respect of the macro-structure and on the mediate level of families – and we could find similar patterns also when looking for instance at provision of social services, the development and structuration of urban spaces, the development of education(al services) etc. Previously individually controlled, though very limited power – limited in terms of scope and reach, however limited also as it had been practical power or 'utility power' – is taken away from the individual's direct control. As such we may see it as matter of increasing societal scope and reach. However as such it is also limited by way of its indirect privatisation. This is not primarily a matter of executing control by individuals.[14] Importantly it is a matter of the interest behind it. And this is determined buy the changing character of power itself. As much as it is originally characterised by its utility character it shifts increasingly towards a constellation where power is – as part of the economic system itself but also as part of the wider soci(et)al fabrique – emerging as matter of 'exchange character'. Paradoxically it is this form of socialisation – that presents a merger between or change over from utility to exchange character (value) – that sets, as its consequence, a process of individualisation free. On another occasion pure individualism had been already characterised and we spoke of

> escalating individualisation, moreover a decoupling of the individual from his/her own personality. Action by individuals is now exactly this: individual action in the sense of isolated acts that are taking mainly place in the sphere of circulation, increasingly independent of processes within the productive sphere. Production and reproduction are left outside, only having meaning as securing existence in a virtual sphere of pure individualism.

> (see Herrmann/Dorrity, 2009: 11 f.)

This gains a new perspective as it is here clearly discernable as inconsistent socialisation.

A matter that should be enforced for focused discussion in this context is the concern for appropriateness – a matter that is already in respect of institutionalist debates relevant as we see from Peter A. Hall's and Rosemary C.R. Taylor's outline who state – after looking in particular at sociological institutionalism - that

> [c]entral to this approach, of course, is the question of what confers 'legitimacy' or 'social appropriateness' on some institutional arrangements but not on others. Ultimately, this is an issue about the sources of cultural authority.

> (Hall/Taylor, 1996: 949)

To elucidate this matter, it is now time to revisit the question of the loss of the commons by highlighting the most important issue of the debate – it is also the most neglected issue or at least one that is not clearly spelled

---

[14] Though this plays a role too, different from society to society and concrete power sharing in different societies.

out. In order of doing so, the following matrix tries to bring schematically together the different dimensions that necessarily need to be addressed.

| | **WILL AND BEHAVIOUR** | | |
	OBJECTIVITY (NORMS)	**ACTUALITY WILL (CONSTITUTION AND BEHAVIOUR)**	**WILL FRAMING (CONDITIONS)**
OWNERSHIP	common	public	private
POWER	collective appropriation	institutionalised as political technology	control and competitive
RIGHTS	based on a tentative and power-based definition of 'justice', guided by a natural and/or divine law	broadly following arguments of legal realism, leaning to and merging with one or the other side of natural/divine law and legal positivism.	following an approach of legal positivism
ACTOR	collective owners	representatives	private contractors
ASSESSMENT	maintenance of commons and exclusive in space/personal attribution ('membership')	commons as public or 'general' interest and 'socially contractualised'; possibly in addition: philanthropy	loss of commons and regulated by private contracts
BASIS FOR 'SOCIAL COHESION' IN THE FRAMEWORK OF GIVEN PROPERTY STRUCTURE	shared practice (see p. 38)	instrumental reason	philanthropy, standing against egoism and hedonism
ADVERSE EXPECTATION IN RELATION TO FORM OF PROPERTY, I.E. WE CANNOT EXPECT:	extensive accumulation and production of (material) wealth	complete avoidance of free-riding	collective responsibility

Table 1

The matrix may give at least some idea about the basic argument: the tenet consists of the shift from immediate control over conditions and actions within the framework of collective shared practice to a setting of individual, formally highly regulated action. Though the first is limited in space and time perspective – and cannot be easily forecasted due to high complexity – the second is able to manage increased space and time, though it is limited by the existence of cut-offs and its individualist structure and also by the unforeseen and/or unintended consequences of ex-post socialisation of the individualist acts. Mentioning the ability of increased space and time control does not mean that the genuinely collective forms have only command over time/space within a limited reach – though it is more a matter of the limitation of the conscious planning of this dimension rather than the actual physical reach. Limitations are surely given also on the 'privatised side' – there being due to patterns of functional reductionism. Between the two extremes we find an intermediary state, aiming on 'bringing the two sides together'. However, it is not a merger in the strict sense. Rather, we are confronted with a distinct pattern of socialisation that is based on a 'new collectivity', namely the interaction of in principal isolated individuals, 'joining forces' by defining contracts as matter of social relationships (of individuals) rather than relations between individuals alone. As such 'new collectivities' they aim not least on inclusion of increased space and time frames into the contractual equations. Depending from where such settings emerge, their shape may be fundamentally different. The problem, then, is obviously the appropriateness of the means in respect of the set societal goals: the loss of the commons is in this light the loss of the commonality of goals and shared action as it can barely be expected that collective responsibility is maintained after the foundation for collective action and shared practice is violently undermined by the acts of primitive accumulation. This is true even if we should not overlook that such violence had been in one or another way the means of braking open the fetters that limited the erstwhile mode of production. – Finally, the question of appropriateness is one of property, namely the correspondence of or clash between the different modes of regulation. If property is private one should definitely not hope for collective responsibility. And if systemic power is based on violence or economic force one should not hope for the other mode to offer compliance. The real tragedy of the commons then is the loss of the common property while the expectation of common decision-making and responsibility *(see on responsibility in more general terms section* Responsibility – Terminological Remarks and Determining the Context*: 40 ff.).*

Simplifying then the statement of Table 1, we arrive at the following matrix for assessment of political-economic systems.[15]

	DECISION-MAKING	RESPONSIBILITY
COLLECTIVE PROPERTY		
PUBLIC PROPERTY		
PRIVATE PROPERTY		

Table 2

This is meant to provide a congruence matrix: Collective forms of property should and can be matched by collective forms of decision-making and responsibility; public forms of property should and can be matched by public forms of decision-making and responsibility; and private forms of property should and can be matched by private forms of decision-making and responsibility. Of course, hybrids can easily be imagined – and can be found in reality. And of course 'should and can' has to be read with consideration: there is some kind of 'private space' also in completely collective and collectivised systems as much as we should not easily use private property systems, allowing them to retreat the social to voluntary action, reducing the understanding of the social to simplify shared practice by reinterpreting it as interaction *(see 38)*. But exactly such property-appropriateness assessment can show the actual systemic flaws, allowing us to avoid looking for romanticist strategies.

At least some empirical evidence for such a shift – and as well for previous integrity – may be given by looking at the development of legal constellations. The general pattern is to look at 'undifferentiated systems', starting from there with the growing division of labour – as social division, including the division of the social being itself – towards highly formalised and abstract systems that emerge (and are constructed) on the basis of functional principles. Though the specifically defined mode of production – as economic system – stands at the centre – another major system in question is the legal system. The interesting point is that with this differentiation we are actually re-entering a circle of traditional forms of socialisation: these functionally differentiated systems – once their borders and codes of communication are set – are now redefining themselves the rules of internal cohesion, inclusion and exclusion etc. . This is a general supposition with view on the economic system. And it is importantly also discussed in regulative systems – the

---

[15] Linking their understanding by leaning boldly towards regulationist approaches.

perpetuation of bureaucracies and the legal system as self-referential and self-reproducing systems are frequently discussed. It is important to see these tendencies of systems to get independent from the societies from which they emerge nevertheless as processes of socialisation or re-socialisation. This coincides with my view on development as oscillation between *'Gemeinschaft'* and 'Gesellsch*aft' (see Herrmann, 2009)*. This position contradicts largely the mainstream understanding of social progress as for instance furthered by Émile Durkheim who can be seen as having set a defining foundation for later reflections on progress and modernisation. According to John Arundel Barnes in Durkheim's work on the division of labour

> *it is asserted that societies may .. be placed on a morphological and at least partly historical continuum. At one end ... are primitive societies; there are characterised by internal differentiation into similar segments with negligible division of labour, legal codes that are mainly repressive, a collective, a collective conscience that predominates in each individual member's mind over the individual component, low moral density, small population and mechanical solidarity. At the other end are higher societies characterised by internal differentiation into many distinct organs, a great division of labour, a legal code that is predominantly concerned with restitutive regulation of inter-personal rights, a collective conscience that constitutes only a modest portion of the mind of each individual, high moral density, a large population and organic solidarity.*

> *(Barnes, J.A., 1966: 166 f.)*

The development is in Durkheim's view not a randomly defined process but

> *a society's movement away from the primitive and towards the higher end of the continuum is due to a causal chain running as follows. A society begins to increase in population and to have a higher population density. Consequently, the struggle for existence becomes more acute and, in order to survive, members of the society develop a division of labour. ... The increasing division of labour then leads to a higher moral density, a decline in the collective component in the conscience, a shift in the structure of the law, and the growth of organic solidarity at the expense of mechanic solidarity.*

> *(ibid.: 167)*

Important is the view from the economic perspective as we find it in the volume on *Global Insights and Explanations* into the *Diversity in Economic Growth (McMahon/Esfahani/Squire (eds.), 2009)*. The authors highlight the fact that we are dealing with complex interrelationships and underline that it is possible to 'ignore the possibility of non-linearities in the growth relationships.' *(ibid. 13)*

One general problem that has to be highlighted again is that the understanding of defining progress actually has no one basis that can be taken for granted and universally or even commonly accepted. Without exploring this further it is at least worthwhile to emphasise that a teleological understanding of progress is surely misleading and it is even more misleading to identify progress with economic growth as for instance suggested when we read Micael Castanheira and Hadi Salehi Eshahani about *Lessons Learned and Challenges Ahead of The Political Economy of Growth,* stating that

> *the political-economy literature studies the role of collective action processes (interest group activity, policy-making institutions, and the like) in resource allocation and rent distribution. The part of that literature that is concerned with economic growth examines the impact of such processes on the incentives of economic agents to invest and to improve productivity in the long run.*
>
> *(Castanheira/Eshahani, 2003: 159; see as well for instance the somewhat self-critical analytical remarks on the Washington Consensus by Robert Zagha/Gobind Nankani and Indermit Gill (Zagha/Nankani/Gill, 2006)*

Having dealt with issue on this occasion in considerable length has one reason that can only now be made explicit. We can see an interesting link between these concrete developments and the shift of power in a very peculiar way that allows us developing a clearer understanding. At first glance we see a shift of power and power holders. Here we can only have a quick look at the two moments. The first is concerned with a shift of power from a simple mechanism of control of others to a more complex power structure that is concerned with the maintenance of the functionality of systems. The second is concerned with the depersonalisation power: Is power in the original instance a matter of personal ownership, this develops increasingly into another direction and emerges depersonalised power *(see Herrmann, Peter, forthcoming b).*[16]

---

[16] It has to be emphasised that this is by no means an absolute development. On the contrary the change also of formal mechanisms as grasped with these shifts, is very much a matter of developing mechanisms that make it possible to maintain the interests which are still very much derived from the traditional patterns of property control.

As result on his investigation of Community Self-Management of Forest in Post-Independence Meghalaya, a State of India as a case of Contested Modernities in an Indigenous Domain, Sanjeeva Kumar comes to the conclusion:

> *What has happened through a process of modernity is co-option of the sub-national state and autonomous units to the meta-narrative of conventional development and simultaneously a process of privatization, aided by a network of actors – well-placed indigenous people and 'non-tribal exploiters from outside', which has weakened the community control.*
>
> *(Kumar, 2007: 30)*

With this in mind he comes importantly to the reasonable request that

> *the relationship of subjects to the environment needs to be examined in their emergence not simply as a part of larger politics by pre-existing interests but more so how the environments and the history of practices in relation to the environment transform actors and interests.*
>
> *(ibid.)*

And with this we can go a huge step further, aiming on developing a sound understanding of the power but more importantly how and in which direction it shifts in a long secular historical perspective.

This means also that the new power structure, as presented and analysed by Sanjeeva Kumar reflects exactly the occurrence of a twofold shift:

(a) From a complex relationship *(α)* between humans and their natural and built environment and *(β)* amongst humans in order to enhance 'relationality and well-being within it' to control over people and possibly enhancing relationality[17] in order of subordination of others *(people and things)* in the interest of private gain.

(b) From an overall pattern of politically defined relationships of power executed through force to a technical relationship – as matter of 'political technology' *(with Foucault)* and as system of utilitarian thought of individually calculated maximisation of greatest happiness.

The actually interesting point is that this reflects exactly the pattern that had been developed above. However, at the same time it underscores the inconsistent character of socialisation. To the extent to which power is 'privatised' in the form of being levered out of the genuine relationality

---

[17] namely in an instrumental way

the change of the 'value of power' as matter of its meaning is transformed into a 'relationship' between individuals that is fundamentally eroded by its exploitative character. It is the replication of the twofold process appearing as political-economic entity presented above *(s. 23)*. However, by looking at Sanjeeva Kumar's case study we see at the same time another crucially important point. The loss of the commons is actually the loss of common power also in terms of the mutuality of the relationship between human and external nature. Thus we extend the argument developed on another occasion where it had been said that

> the loss of the commons as guiding the moral standard appears as having a much more central role as the frequently deplored loss of communitarian spirit.
>
> *(Herrmann, Peter, 2010 (a))*

We can push this now a little bit further by saying that the actual loss of the commons is one of loosing common control *(due to privatisation)* and moreover, it is a loss of common or shared practice to the extent to which practice is reduced on action and relations are reduced on interaction of isolated, 'independent' individuals as described by Slife. If we look with Barry Barnes at shared practices, acknowledging that

> [t]hey are indeed not stable unitary essences, but neither are they clusters of habitual individual actions. Shared practices are the accomplishments of competent members of collectives. They are accomplishments readily achieved by, and routinely to be expected of members acting together, but they nonetheless have to be generated on every occasion, by agents concerned all the time to retain coordination and alignment with each other in order to bring them about
>
> *(Barnes, Barry, 2001: 32 f.)*

we clearly see what happened: the enclosure as violent appropriation of common property by private 'entrepreneurs' meant also the undermining of shared practice – in this sense we see indeed a loss of the commons. It is not least a loss of the commons in terms of the loss of an understanding of rights as matter of shared practice and their transformation into formal, legislative systems. As such, it is very much the replication of the transformation of power from having been a pattern of appropriation of situations to power as matter of control over people. This should not make us overlooking that such development is characterised by alienation on the one hand but also by an increased objectification: accountability, universality not also adaptability to difference and accommodation of diversity. Finally we should not forget that historically – despite all lamentable closure of today's societies, we still have gained more openness than those closed communitarian systems of the past. In this sense the option is not the wistful, romanticising look back but the necessity to appropriate the current opportunities, i.e. to avail of property rights over the enhanced means of (re-)[production. Other options end too easily in the deadlock of rebirth of fundamentalism – including fundamentalism from Christianity.

Coming back to what Michel Foucault said about the political technology we can now see that it is not necessarily the question of reflexive perspective that is taken *(the orientation of state action, i.e. governing)* on maintaining itself. Rather, it is about the establishment of 'new hegemons' by capping rationalities from their complex prerogatives, transforming them into limited ones. As much as this can be a matter of establishing self-referential systems, it can also (and much more so) be a matter of applying 'alien standards' as we see it in many cases happening: the dominance of bureaucratic rule, the supremacy of 'economic thinking',[18] and the like. – And of course, here we are back to works of Max Weber on rationalisation, Antonio Gramsci on hegemony and so many other thinkers of social science.[19]

Leaning towards legal terminology we can also say that we are – entwisting both patterns – facing the development from in the widest sense morally defined systems of justice to technically defined systems of legality *(see in this context for the latter for instance the works of Niklas Luhmann and Gunther Teubner on reflexivity of modern legal systems).*

Although all this is analytical rather than providing a descriptive retrospect, we should not fall into the trap which already holds so many corpses of thought that deflagrated in the radiance of enlightenment: The picture is not one of a better or worse scenario; rather it is a simple tracing of some main strokes which are so often forgotten by the brush led by the modernist social scientists of Cartesian descent.[20]

---

[18] which, we should never forget this, is meant to characterise a very specific understanding of what 'economics' is about.

[19] See in this context as well Hall/Taylor, 1996

[20] All this does not want to provide a bright picture that forgets the contradictions, inequalities and injustices of the past and as much as we should not get caught in the Cartesian pitfalls we have to avoid any romantisation too.

Smart Socio-Economies – Continued

But social integrity meant as well social closure: a system based on ascribing and inheriting positions rather than following some kind of meritocracy rules. i.e. rules of obtaining positions on grounds of ability and skills. – Shallow societies with two dimensions: here and now.

Sure, we should not have illusions – it had been a shallow society as well: if you look at the painting you see two dimensions – not more. The hunters and gatherers had not been able to paint spatial dimensions not because arts had not yet been sufficiently developed. The reason had been another: sight hasn't been sufficiently developed: sight – as matter of thinking, as matter of grasping dimensions – had been geared towards the here and now. It had been the engagement with the immediate environment. Of course, within these remits, within this space dimensions had been added – and actually they had been added in a most skilful, adept way. And this meant not least, in a most responsible way. We can see this is in the skilful work not least of the Egypt region where craftpeopleship and arts developed in extremely high, though primitive ways.

Responsibility – Terminological Remarks and Determining the Context

Responsible?

Let us briefly look at the term and play a little with it, deconstructing its common meaning of moral accountability. There are in particular the two elements in it:

- "Re-" as matter of "return" and
- "spondere" as pledge.

However, another element comes to mind – though etymologically such reference is not fully justified. But it still makes much sense when it comes to understanding responsibility: rather than reading "re" we can read "res", translated, of course, into thing, matter, affair. And whenever we look at responsibility as providing a response we arrive at marking a crucial relationship between at least three elements, (i) the matter in question, i.e. a part of any reality we look at, (ii) the purpose of our dealing with it, (iii) the way in which we are dealing with it. In other words, the responsibility is not a neutral instance nor is it an instance that finds its reason only in the object itself. In any case, it is a matter of understanding the meaning that is inherent in the matter we look at and the meaning that is given by our relationship to it. This is of crucial importance whenever we think scientifically – and it is the most commonly forgotten issue when it comes to academic practice: there we reduce this complex relationship, defining it on the one hand as relationship between researcher and financier and on the other hand as relationship between researcher and object. In any case, the problem is that we are not dealing with a complex relationship of societal practice. This fall of mankind is not a matter of recent developments only but can be followed way back: in a fundamentally individualist stance coming along with the so-called enlightenment to the extent to which this had been based in the original accumulation and the subsequent emergence of private contracts as the fundamental means of constituting social relationships – and we will surely come back to it at a later stage.

So far, from all this it should get clear that we have to be very careful when it comes to dealing with responsibility. First, it is important to think of responsibility as a dynamic matter rather than a matter of a static relationship. And second it is just this: a relationship that has to be developed in the fullest sense.

Provisionally we may see it as relationship between a (i) given reality – or the research object, (ii) our own interest or the interest of the financing instance – the stance of the researcher and (iii) the actual research as matter of methodology and methods. It does not take much effort to translate this trinity as reflection of the other trinity which had been outlined above: the trinity of individualism, elitism and not least the founding theodicy.

And in this Holy Trinity of research there is nothing independent of the other. And though of course natural and even social reality exists as such, it is as research object at the same time depending on our intervention, be it only by fact of selection. – Towards the end this will be explored a little bit further: looking at engagement and disengagement.

And coming back to the hunters and gatherers: from what we know they had been only using so much of the resources which had been necessary – necessary for the moment. Apparently, people did not believe that "god will fix". They believed in the moment – shallow, limited, not really being able to go beyond the given space – not seeing spaces and not even seeing the full range of the space that had been open before them. Crucial to understand this stage of development is to find time and action as immediate entity.

When I said "god had a plan" it had been of course a statement of relative truth: in these predominantly pagan – and not god-depending – societies "gods plan" had been the plan of things themselves. Much later, in the 1950, the German philosopher Max Horkheimer, talked about objective and subjective reason – the first being the reason that is inherent to the matter, the second

> *dealing predominantly with the relation between means and ends, with the appropriateness of procedural rules in respect to the aims, which themselves are more or less accepted, without being questioned in terms of their own rationality.*

> *(Horkheimer, 1952: 5f.)*

Smart and Shallow – Early Economies

In these early societies reason could only be objective:

- a matter of human beings directly interacting with nature and
- a matter of power that developed from here: the power in the sense of pouvoir, of abilities, of mastering

And with this a society which had been called by Samir Amin tributary society *(see Amin, 1989),* a society which may be with all qualifications characterised by the famous words of Karl Marx used for characterising a much later, higher phase of society, a phase

> *... after the enslaving subordination of the individual to the division of labour, and thereby also the antithesis between mental and physical labour, has vanished; after labour has become not only a means of life but life's prime want; after the productive forces have also increased with the all-around development of the individual, and all the springs of common wealth flow more abundantly – only then can the narrow horizon of bourgeois right be crossed in its entirety and society inscribe on its banners: From each according to his ability, to each according to his needs!*

> *(Marx, 1875: 87)*

Sure, they had been responsible societies as they did only act within these two dimensions.

There are two implications – apparently simple but with grave consequences:

First, the split of reason: on the one hand instrumental, subjective reason and on the other hand objective reason had not taken place at this stage:

though (or because?) reason had been limited, it had been characterised by its entity.

Getting the Ball Rolling

Second, and quite dramatically for the development of power, the worldview had been ... – well, nothing else: centred on the world, even more: seeing the world as centre.

Illustration 3[21]

As said, this had been of decisive meaning for the development of power – and here I am not speaking of power as ability but as power of execution of force. The role of the Roman-Catholic church had been one point in question – and surely it is problematic to use the past tense, as it is an ongoing power. It had been only this year that an important document had been published:

---

[21]   Source: Peter Herrmann

Illustration 4[22]

– and it had been only in 1992 that the catholic church opened the doors again for Galilee Galileo. Mind, all this had been very much a global feature, something that we can find in all corners of the early world rather then being a European phenomenon: China as the Middle Kingdom, the Islam world, especially as it developed in Egypt and leaving only few areas out of such global realm: those societies that remained organised according to the principals of contributions, i.e. being in the words of Samir Amin tributary societies (see Amin, 1989). With this it is, of course, suggested that the world system exists 5000 rather than only 500 years *(see Gills/Frank, 1993)*.

But there had been another issue that had been equally important when it comes to power. All this had been closely linked to a mechanical model in thinking – and it had been on this basis, this mechanical worldview, that space could be and had to be explored. In a way still a golden age: the age of people dealing with each other, directly, within such tributary system. And although power surely had been frequently misused, it had been a time and space that had been manageable, self-sufficient. Long chains of interdependence did not really exist – instead it had been the old patterns of direct control. And this had been in one way or another a politically defined and legitimised power relationship.

---

[22]   Source: Peter Herrmann

The reproduction of the precapitalist social systems rests upon the stability of power (which is the basic concept defining the domain of the political) and of an ideology that endows it with legitimacy. In other words, politico-ideological authority (the 'superstructure') is dominant at this point.

(Amin, 1989: 2)

A golden age as well in terms of astonishing beauty – if you could ever have a look at the cupola of the duomo in Florence you will know what I mean: an amazing view from the ground and still being multiplied when walking so to say through the fresco. You will know what I mean when you have seen the Palazzo Vecchio – a monument highlighting the turn away from the medieval ages and arriving at the renaissance. A time overcoming slowly but surely the understanding of the world being flat. Two paradoxes occurred. The first can be seen in Michelangelo's famous piece The Creation of Adam.

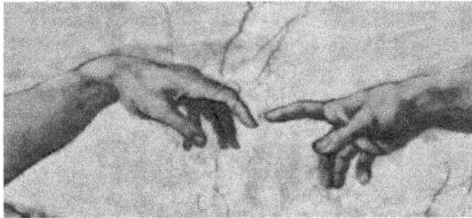

Illustration 5[23]

You can read it in different ways – and one version is that god finally dethroned herself – knowing about the work by Nicolaus Copernicus, Galilee Galileo and Giordano Bruno. Be it is it is, new possibilities and forces had been developing with respect to responsibility:

Coming back to playing with different possible dimensions contained in the term responsibility we arrive at another possible element: the Latin pondere. Here the linguistic dimension is about balance, even equilibrium and at least weighing, considering and reflecting.

Supposedly Michelangelo's David had been the first statue that stood, truly balancing the weight by its own perfection, truly taking power over a three-dimensional space.

---

[23] http://upload.wikimedia.org/wikipedia/commons/d/d3/Michelangelo_Buonarroti _017.jpg; 10.08.2012

Renaissance – the Birth of the Individual

David had been one the most impressive pieces of art of this age. Another masterpiece of the time had been Gian Lorenzo Bernini's Il Ratto di Proserpina

Illustration 6[24]

– today you can see it Galleria Borghese. This statue is so impressive because it captures the third dimension in a unique way – and if you stand in front of it, if you walk around it, there is something else opening up in front of your eyes: an entirely new responsibility – understood in terms of engaging, of responding to the world. Actually, a rather complex feature is emerging; a new response – but required and at the same time only possible by a new way of capturing reality: The third dimension – you can also see them in the most exciting way when looking at the fresco by Tommaso Maria Conca and the decorations by Giovanni Battista Marchetti – is not only the opening of space as being perfectly reproducible. With this, two other moments come into play: time and feeling.

---

[24] http://www.omero.it/media/79/20070902-3.%20Ratto%20di%20Proserpina.jpg; 10.08.2012

Time and feeling are of course in there own terms most complex issues and I want to point only on one of them: the Renaissance as the Naissance – the birth of individuality. And we can go so far that it had been this specific kind of individuality that made it possible and necessary that Galileo finally said

Tamensi Movetur

Illustration 7

"Eppur si muove!" – "And yet it [the earth] moves."

It had been an individuality that had been based in the fundamental separation between economic life, political control and individuality of civil life – a separation of which the consequence can be seen until today: as matter of analysing state, economy and civil society, as distinguishing social and civil dialogue as partnering towards the political system or as well as the separation that stands at the centre of this presentation's attention: as well the separation between science, social science and reality. Understanding this process in a concise way requires also recognising this development as a reflection of an ambivalent societal development that is on the one hand concerned with personification as process of allowing the development of an independent personality, however that encapsulates the reification of the 'independent and hedonist individual' that is then apparently acting independently. Part of this is not least that reification actually means that the personality development is getting caught in systemic structures that emerged as independent 'agencies' in their own right.[25]

A golden age of huge developments and a most brutal era – perhaps more brute than the middle ages. The new dimensions of space and subsequently time and individual feeling meant the conscious use of violence, the acceptance of suffering of the other – look at Bernini's Proserpina and you can see from where she comes, and how she feels: even in the cold stone work you see warmth. A time where Galileo's suffering had been equally and consciously accepted as the Machiavelli's

---

[25] In this context of interest is the evaluation of the development *From Objective to Subjective Law,* brought forward by Verschraegen *(see Verschraegen, 2002; in particular 264 f.)*

tortures, being victim of the power quarrels of the "bad princes" and the suffering of hundreds and thousands of people whose meagre accommodation had been demolished, their lives destroyed by the power obsession of the Medici in building the palace at the Piazza della Signoria – mind: a space for the new democracy. And as much as god handed power down, it had been the catholic church that stood over all this, still gaining from the situation: The world stood in the centre, had been the centre – and this justified the maintenance of a central power: the power of the church itself. But it had been as well the justification of competition amongst individuals and it had been a time of huge progress in science. The heading can be kept short: the manufacturability of the world.

May be that it had been somewhat blaspheme – but as Protestantism still stood only on the doorsteps this had not been a real problem. The church knew how to live with contradictions.

Illustration 8[26]

And so it accepted delights – paradise lost, but still present, obtainable.

Of course this could not be maintained forever – rationality moved further; and we arrive at another paradox:

---

[26] http://commons.wikimedia.org/wiki/File:The_Garden_of_Earthly_Delights_ by_Bosch_High_Resolution.jpg; 10.08.2012

Disenchantment – The Emergence of Joyless Individuals

Moving away from the irrationality meant the emergence of a new irrationality – Max Weber extensively described and analysed this "Entzauberung der Welt" – the disenchantment; turning Karl Marx on his head: the latter pointed already on the close connection between protestant ethics and capitalism but emphasised that capitalism stood behind Protestantism rather than the other way round. At this point another issue is of more importance:

Illustration 9[27]

Disenchantment did not primarily mean the development of new responsibilities. Rather, now we see the completion of the disengagement of subjective reason from objective reason. We are dealing with a long period over which developments took place. One moment of this had been the development of universities which began – with some qualifications – in the Middle Ages. Rightly, this had been frequently emphasised as the development of institutions that dealt with the entirety of human knowledge, bringing together (or at least claiming and aiming on bringing together) universal knowledge, i.e. knowledge of the universe. But equally it meant to gather and provide "knowledge for all" – a small error in writing the reality of history happened: liberté, égalité, fraternité developed towards liberty for a selected number of citizens only – in this sense nothing had been new. However, democratisation

---

[27] Source: Peter Herrmann

cannot be denied and part of it was that education had been generalised. And as much as we may complain about slide-presentations and blackboard as part of an overall managerialist strategy which is fundamentally geared towards accepting reality as unchangeable but being threatened by an "outer world", we can question if the model of the time had been much better. What looks quite amusing so far, does look less amusing if we look at what it actually was

Illustration 10[28]

perhaps to some of you known under the term Nuernberger Trichter.

Re-Christianisation

A remark in passing: although all this is usually seen as undermining the role of religion such stance can well be contested: Protestantism, now developing even to state religions in some countries, could develop a much stronger grip, subordinating humankind under the notion of this-worldliness. Now religion required unfailingly a devote life – the joys which could easily be compensated for by praying had been lost. A

---

[28] http://fh-bi.ia20xx.de/wp-content/uploads/2010/10/Nuernberger_Trichter-193x300.jpg; 10.08.2012

joyless society emerged – and this may allow for the play with words in German language where joy translates into Freud(e): over short or long the Freud-less society made it necessary to develop a Freud-full psychology: psychoanalysis trying to deal with the consequences of strict repression. Sure, Catholicism had not necessarily been a psychological cure but at least confession did not need a professional analyst or therapist – a priest could do the same job and the danger of catholic liberation theology, as real as it had been throughout the centuries had been less likely to emerge as profound soci(et)al power than the emergence of a protestant or even secular liberation movement. And another consideration is useful: As much as we face – at least on the level of appearance – in particular in countries as Ireland, Italy or Spain processes of secularisation, we have to acknowledge at the same time opposite trends (see for instance Sweeney, 2008; Wallace, 1966; as well Herrmann, Peter, forthcoming a). What stands for investigation is the following: Richard Sennett draws the attention to

> the erosion of Protestant Ethic ... in the realm of personal strategic planning.

> (Sennett, 2006: 79)

Referring to a study by Michael Laskaway (see Laskaway, 2004) he compares

> the career planning of young adults in the 1970s to those today. Both groups are university-educated and ambitious; the striking difference between them is how there ambitions are focused. The group from an earlier generation thought in terms of long-term strategic gains, the contemporary group in terms of their immediate prospects. More finely, the older group was able to verbalize goals, whereas the contemporary group had trouble finding a language to match their impulses. In particular, the older group could define its eventual gratifications, while the contemporary group dealt with in more amorphous desires.

> (Sennett: ibid.)

And such pattern of re-catholised mindsets fits perfectly into the development of economy and politics. It is the re-emerging dominance of the sphere of circulation as apparent source of huge values (as we can see it as pattern preceding capitalism; see Herrmann, forthcoming a). And the re-emergence of the Prince – entirely a modern form of the Machiavellian figure, being at times a generous benefactor after availing of profits from inconceivable speculation-based gains; and being able and willing to live easily along the lines of paradoxes, even advertising them in seemingly and occasionally macabre post-modern fashion:

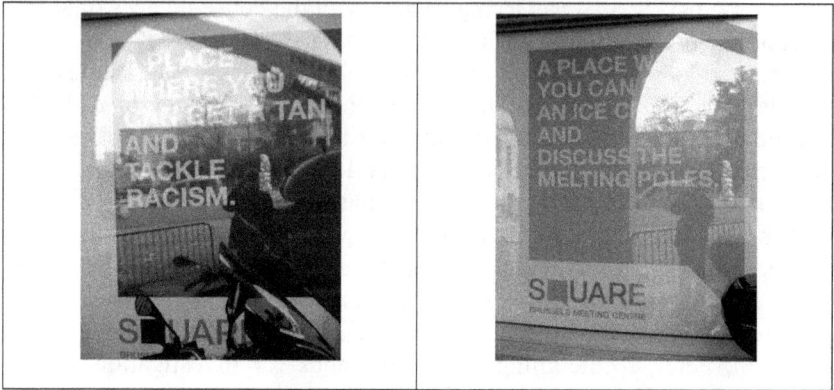

Illustration 11[29]

A Place Where You can Get A Tan And Tackle Racism; A Place Where You Can Enjoy An Ice Cream And Discuss The Melting Poles; A Place Where You Can Sit In The Shadows And Stand In The Spotlight; A Place Where you Can Eat Sandwiches And Fight World Hunger.[30]

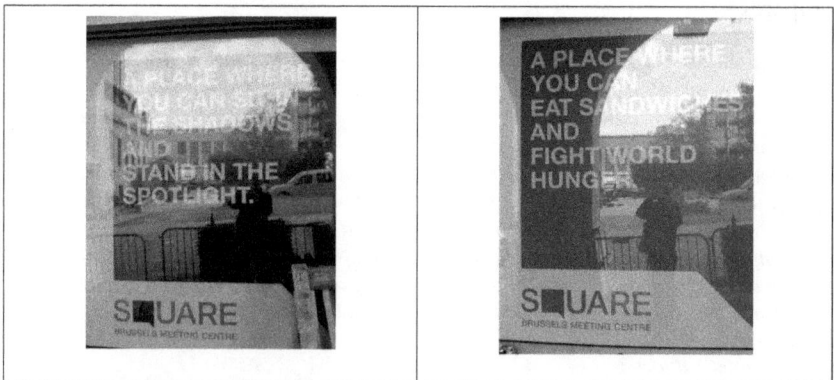

Illustration 12[31]

---

[29] Source: Peter Herrmann
[30] Alluding to posters in Brussels which accompanied in September 2009 the opening of "The Square" - Brussels Meeting Centre.
[31] Reference: Peter Herrmann

Construction and De-Construction – Paradoxes of Emerging Trade-Societies

Let me come back to the title of this presentation: Science – Social Science – Practice or: Searching for Responsibility. I dealt somewhat explicit with defining responsibility. Let me now turn to the term science – the Latin roots are twofold: on the one hand reference has to be made to scire: knowing; and at the same time we are dealing with scindere: to separate. To some extent the second dimension is an epistemological question: availing of knowledge by separation, by deconstruction and reconstruction and new construction.

It is from here that being responsible gains a new perspective: the inherent challenge to be responsible to its own rationality. This development occurred, of course, in strict contradiction to what Immanuel Kant, one of the great thinkers of the enlightenment said, defining this as

> *man's emergence from his self-imposed immaturity. Immaturity is the inability to use one's understanding without guidance from another. This immaturity is self-imposed when its cause lies not in lack of understanding, but in lack of resolve and courage to use it without guidance from another. Sapere Aude! [dare to know] "Have courage to use your own understanding!" -- that is the motto of enlightenment.*

> *(Kant, 1784)*

It had been as well during this time that the split between science and social science became more pronounced and more obscuring. What can probably be said in terms of space is the following: first the emerging and increasingly domineering orientation towards details.

Illustration 13 [32]

One of the masterpieces of this "space" is Rembrandt Harmenszoon van Rijn's "Night Watch".

The real content is the strictness – have a close look and you can see everything being well ordered: everybody having a position and everybody's position actually marked by a very relationship to a specific part of the environment: traders, politicians, producers found – in general – their place in the paintings of Rembrandt and his paining company. And mind: I say company as the era of schools as they dominated the time of Leonardo da Vinci had forgone.

The second point worth to be mentioned is the emerging and increasingly accepted orientation towards reality. Finally reality did have changed. The ancient citizen had been the only class that counted and rather homogenous; the new citizen: the citoyen from the French Revolution had been open, being an individual but as well part of a diverse people. It had been a time

> *of respect, of rights, of dignity. Consider the meaning and emotion packed into the French citoyen of 1789, a word that condemned tyranny and social hierarchy, while affirming self-government and status equality; that was a moment when even women succeeded in claiming address as citoyenne rather than as madam or mademoiselle.*
>
> *(Fraser/Gordon: 90)*

We may say that the Protestantism meant the emergence of burgher. And as much as the burgher enjoyed being celebrated, he enjoyed being

---

[32] http://www.zeno.org/Kunstwerke.images/I/kml5047a.jpg; 10.08.2012

celebrated for being celebrated as responsibly acting. And we should not forget: this burgher had been fighting as much against an ancient regime as the citoyen: against feudal structures and a specific form of the guild system. – Pictures of the time that are commonly not so well known are for instance Rembrandt's paintings of the anatomy lesson of professor Nicolaes Tulp and similar. Again, at least fine arts felt in many times still too fine to look at other parts of reality – the reality that had been seen as error of history: the reality that fundamentally contradicted the ideologically tainted version in Gottfried Keller's novel Jeder ist seines eigenen Glueckes Schmied – Everyone is his owns luck forger. It had been the further development: the upcoming dominance of the hitherto somewhat hidden, in some way dormant bourgeois.

It is here that what is entailed in Niklas Luhmann's dictum comes to the full blossom, namely that everything could be different but nothing can be done.

But – you may expect already that I come up with it – a paradox again. On the one hand we find in social science – lead by economics – the loss of objective rationality and even the loss of the social: Jeremy Bentham and John Stuart Mills brought forward utilitarianism: an entirely rational system, the attempt to calculate happiness which right today peaks in Joseph Stiglitz' considerations on "Well-being Matters in Measuring Social Progress" (see Stiglitz, 2009); if we take it epistemologically: Adam Smith insisting on a similar approach and bringing forward economics on the one hand and supplementing it by a moral philosophy which he positioned outside of the economic realm – sure, he could not be entirely consistent with such separation but the epistemological ground had been this. As stated on various other occasions: the new society finally emerged … - well, actually Margaret Thatcher had been in some way correct, saying there is no such thing as society (see Thatcher, 1987). She had been correct insofar as the economic school she followed had been rather successful in dismantling society, destroying the ideals of the revolution: *liberté, égalité, fraternité* by consequently following its objective reasoning: reinterpreting the liberty of rights into the freedom of contracts, the redefinition of equality on the basis of exchange and the understanding of fraternity in its capitalised form: as matter of social capital. – The underlying problem being expressed by Georges Soros who speaks of transactions having replaced relationships in people's dealing with one another *(see Soros, 1998).*

Advancement of Science – And Falling Back

On the other hand we find science, now split from social science. This allowed a huge progress: the world had not been left in the centre of the universe simply because god and the worldly representatives wanted so; the world could be put into place by simply detecting and following the rules of its objective existence and location: the split can in some way be seen as gaining a holistic view (and I do not have to say that this is another paradox), not least by finally even sequencing the DNA. However, loosing the link to the social and social thinking showed colossal negative effects: the loss of the subject meant that the object emerged itself as subject.

– In a nutshell one person stands for the entire drama of the development: Albert Einstein. Genius, disengaged and perhaps we may say obsessed by science – separating even reality from itself, so to say making it relative. And although he clearly saw from there that everything is relative, i.e. as well a matter of relating to a given society, it needed the practice: the Unites States violently and destructively utilising this knowledge to make him from one of the most irresponsible scientists to one of the most responsible scientifically informed social actors.

Having been rather critical towards my own profession, I have to qualify this. Of course, there had been those who did never go this way of allowing departmentalisation: who continued to emphasise the importance of grand theories or grand narratives as it is called nowadays, aiming on keeping the different strands of (social) science integrated. There are different approaches to it, reaching from emphasising interdisciplinary approaches to generically integrated approaches as e find them for instance in the field of world-systems theory.

A useful starting point for further considerations may be a statement, made by Sir Anthony Atkinson who had been recently guest speaker in Cork at the Department of Applied Social Studies. On the occasion of the Brussels Economic Forum he had been asked 'In what respects are economists to blame?' and of course the concern had been the blame taken for the current crisis: a crisis of the financial markets, a recession of the productive sectors, a crisis of the social security systems and a crisis of living together. And his answer had been simple – and due to its simplicity such statement is easily pushed aside. He said:

> *I believe that economists can be rightly criticised for having become over-specialised. It is quite reasonable for the subject to be divided into micro-economics and macro-economics, but we have seen it become*

increasingly sub-divided and fragmented. People only study a particular form of macro-economics; they specialise in a particular approach, such as DSGE modelling. In these fields they attain high levels of technical expertise, but they are not able to react flexibly as circumstances require. Academic economists have come to resemble highly-bred race horses, trained to race on the flat over a certain distance, but not able to jump over fences and still less to pull a plough. Economists are good in their niche, but unable to cope with a changing environment.

(Atkinson, 2009: 21)

Searching for Prosponsibility

I am coming to the end – not least as what is necessary now is a complete second presentation: the exploration of another paradox and for me it is the most difficult on, of course, as I am in the middle of it. The problem is not only that we have to overcome the split between the different strands of science. More important is actually that we need a new responsibility – as much as we have a new reality.

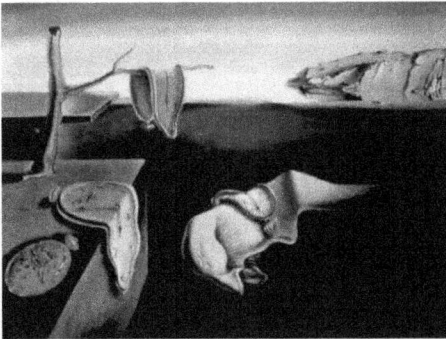

Illustration 14 [33]

I do not want to look at the many things which had been said about the so-called postmodern societies, the somewhat antagonistic tension between the "panoptisme", i.e. panoptic surveillance as mentioned by Michel Foucault (see Foucault, 1975) on the one hand and liquid modernity, using the title of a book by Zygmunt Bauman *(see Bauman, 2000).*

---

[33] http://mywritestuff.blogs.the-dispatch.com/files/2011/07/the_persistence_of_memory_-_1931_salvador_dali-1.jpg; 10.08.2012

Instead I want to look at the – currently – main challenge: responsibility. As said before, responsibility is mainly about two things: (i) "Re-" as matter of "return" and "spondere" as accepting a pledge and (ii) responsiveness, as responding to a given situation and matter, responding to a reality. For whichever reason this reality seems to be fluid, changing. I want to point on four moments that I consider as centrally important:

- increasing complexity – and this means not least the knowledge of complexity;

- increasing engagement as matter of being able to change things (though mind that everything could be different but we are not able to change things);

- increasing engagement as matter of gaining the ability of determining the direction of change and the way of changing: the overall secular move from static-circular reproduction to reproductive production to changing production and finally now the – seemingly – independent creation;

- decreasing of the social, to some extent immediately linked to general patterns for enlightenment, to a much larger extent linked to a very specific societal form of production that emerged from there.

The problem – and it is again a paradoxical one – is that on the one hand we need to engage, to orient our action on answering the immediate needs of the here and now: you may see it as high price we have to pay for the loss of god though I would see it as huge gain. On the other hand, it is disengagement that actually secures science as matter of knowing (scire) and separating (scindere).

And being social scientist myself I may remind us of Norbert Elias' critique

> ... I have so far omitted to mention is fear of the unknown and thus of innovations. One has sometimes the impression that in recent times sociologists no longer expect that one can make basic discoveries in their field of work. ...
>
> A high level of involvement paralyses the capacity for encapsulated discovery.
>
> (Elias, 1986: 22)

This is, of course, a complex issue – and Richard Sennett states fro example in the book already quoted:

58

The more one understands how to do something well, the more one care about it. Institutions based on short-term transactions and constantly shifting tasks, however, do not breed that depth. Indeed the organization can fear it; the management code work is ingrown. Someone who digs deep into an activity just to get it right can seem to others ingrown in the sense of fixated on that one thing – and obsession is indeed necessary for the craftsman. He or she stands at the opposite pole from the consultant, who swoops in and out but never nests.

(Sennett, op.ct.: 105)

The actual challenge is here actually manifold, and one important thing is the historical dimension again: On the one hand the engagement with the object itself requires engagement: a high degree without which 'production' is not possible and this may be the production of a seemingly simple thing as a beautifully crafted chair or the production of the impossible[34]: the social. On the other hand, such engagement hinders us to get the distance to actually change things, the latter requiring disengagement – the disenchantment of the beauty and ugliness of the presence. However, what presents itself as contradiction in terms is actually only the paradox of levels. Change needs equally engagement but its requires to engage on a different, higher level and it also requires to engage on different levels at the same time. We are actually confronted with the dialectical relationship between the concrete, general, abstract and specific.

As well, we have to be exceedingly careful when approaching this topic as the question of involvement and detachment may well be seen in close connection with the question of value freedom – the question of neutrality of the (social) scientist – and though a lengthy debate took place, indissolubly connected with names as Wilhelm Dilthey, Heinrich Rickert, Max Weber, Werner Sombart and Gustav Schmoller and later famously taken up in particular by Theodor Adorno during the 16th congress of the German Sociological Association in 1969 – debates known under the heading Werturteilsstreit (the dispute on value freedom), we have to be careful. Of course, there is this dimension of values linked to the exploration of involvement and detachment. However, there is also the other side in it: if we allow ourselves being caught in applying solely instrumental reason we are permanently engaged in certain presupposed values

---

[34] Allegedly Niklas Luhmann – but others did so before in similar veins – said that the functioning of the social would be extremely unlikely.

At the end, the reality we face allows us – and urges us – now to overcome the holy trinity of the father, the son and the holy spirit, the trinity of reality, social science and science. Historically we find the development of a four dimensional space of action: the overall secular move

- from static-circular reproduction – the 2-dimensional space,
- to reproductive production – the three-dimensional space,
- to changing production as profit-oriented, instrumentally lead society – the one-dimensional space *(cf. Marcuse, 1964)*,
- and finally now the – seemingly – independent creation: a matter of introducing a fourth dimension; and as current challenge of answering increasing complexity, the ability to change things and determining the direction of change by re-introducing the social on a higher level.

Illustration 15[35]

Surely a major challenge as time has to be considered as a major issue but needs doing so by going fundamentally beyond the individualist dimension as it is typical for surrealist views. It is about social time, ergo requiring the re-establishment of the social-social (rather than an abstract social individual). We arrive at another paradox: It means to move away from a moral understanding of what a good society may be and how we can define rights (see on the latter: Herrmann, the contributions "Rights-Based Approaches Against Social Injustice – Putting Social Law into

---

[35] http://hinter-den-schlagzeilen.de/wp-content/uploads/2012/04/Guernica-300x178.jpg; 10.08.2012

Perspective" and "Justice and Law today: On the translation of general ideas on justice into claims for security and responsibility" in this volume). Pablo Picasso – on occasion of the bitter experience at Guernica – depicted one side of it: evil as real possibility. It is not only the evil of the violent intervention and the consequences for individuals. Moreover, we face the cubist dimension – the variability that builds and potentially destroys the social. In the words used by Pablo Picasso: "Every positive value has its price in negative terms... the genius of Einstein leads to Hiroshima." *(http://www.brainyquote.com/quotes/ authors/p/pablo_picasso.html - 04/11/2009 11:31 a.m.)*

A fact that surrealism with its by and large individualist orientation could not cope with as social fact, not being able to face reality like postmodernism is by and large not able to face reality: both, surrealism and postmodernism generate themselves as annex to an forgone history.

And rather taking another example of Pablo Picasso, we can come with now two paintings by Odilon Redon offering other important perspectives.

It is about the appropriation of movement and processes:

Illustration 16[36]

---

[36] http://upload.wikimedia.org/wikipedia/commons/4/4b/Odilon_Redon_002.jpg, 10.08.2012

and the conflation with space:

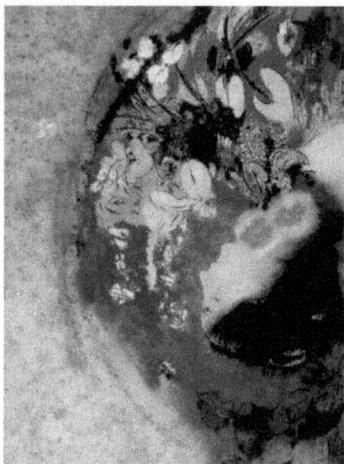

Illustration 17[37]

After accepting the – potential – reality of evil and after moving away from a moral reasoning for the social we have to move on by looking at a positive understanding of the social, based on the engagement with – social and natural – space *(see as well Herrmann/Herrenbrueck, 2007 a, b)*.

To bring things back in line we should consider understanding

- responsibility – answering – not least as matter of prosponsible: a pledge for the future and

- emphasise scire – the matter of knowing rather than looking at the promotion of skills as matter of scindere: the separation.

All this is, of course, not least a matter of reconsidering as well – in a responsible and prosponsible way – what we have to understand as possible (see for instance the elaboration by Ernst *Bloch (see Bloch, 1959: 258-288)*.

---

[37]   http://upload.wikimedia.org/wikipedia/commons/f/fc/Odilon_Redon_-
       _Ophelia.JPG; 10.08.2012

Illustration 18[38]

In such situation we have to avoid one thing – as scientists, as social scientists or as universalists of any couleur: pretending innocence. What ever we do, i.e. in which ever way we are accepting and changing practice – we are responding – we are responsible for what we are doing and there is no way to claim innocence of little angels. And this is true if we act or if we act by allowing others to act.

---

[38] http://www.channelingheaven.com/wp-content/uploads/2011/09/michelangelo-angels.jpg; 10.08.2012

References

Amin, Samir, 1989: Eurocentrism; New York: Monthly Review Press

Amin, Samir, 2008: Du Capitalisme à la Civilisation. La Longue Transition; Paris: Éditions Syllepse

Apthorpe, Raymond, 1997: Human Development and Social Anthropology; in: Social Anthropology; Edited by the European Association of Social Anthropologists; 5,1: 21-34

Atkinson, Anthony B.: Three questions about the global economic crisis and three conclusions for EU and Member State policy-makers; in: European Commission. Directorate General for Economic and Financial Affairs (Ed.): Beyond the Crisis: A Changing Economic Landscape. Keynote Speeches at the Brussels Economic Forum 2009; ECFIN Economic Brief; 2. June 2009: 21-32

Barnes, Barry, 2001: Practice as Collective Action; in: Schatzki, Theodore R./Knorr-Cetina, Karin/von Savigny, Eike (eds.): The Practice Turn in Contemporary Theory; London: Routledge: 25-36

Barnes, J.A., 1966: Durkheim's Division of Labour in Society; in: Man (New Series), 1/2 (Jun): 158-175; Published by: Royal Anthropological Institute of Great Britain and Ireland; Stable URL: http://www.jstor.org/stable/2796343, Accessed: 06/07/2010 19:14

Barroso, José Manuel, 2009: Political Guidelines for the Next Commission; September 2009: 2 - http://ec.europa.eu/commission_barroso/president/pdf/press_20090903_EN.pdf - 05/10/2009 5:16 p.m.

Bauman, Zygmunt, 2000: Liquid Modernity; Cambridge: Cambridge University Press

Benedict XVI, 2009: Caritas in Veritate; Vatican: Libreria Editrice Vaticana, 2009

Bloch, Ernst, 1959: Prinzip Hoffnung; Frankfurt/M: Suhrkamp [written in 1938-1947; reviewed 1953 and 1959]

Bourdieu, Pierre, 1983: Ökonomisches Kapital, kulturelles Kapital, soziales Kapital; in: Soziale Ungleichheiten (Soziale Welt, Sonderheft 2), edited by Reinhard Kreckel. Goettingen: Otto Schartz & Co.: 183-198

Bourdieu, Pierre, 1986: The Forms of Capital, in: John G. Richardson (Ed.): Handbook of Theory and Research in the Sociology of Education, New York/N.Y. & London: Greenwood Press: 241-258

Braudel, Fernand, 1967 et altera: Civilisation matérielle, économie et capitalisme (XVe-xviiie siècle); Paris Armand Colin

Castanheira, Micael/Eshahani, Hadi Salehi, 2003: The Political Economy of Growth. Lessons Learned and Challenges Ahead; in: McMahon, Gary/Squire, Lyn. The global Development Network (eds.): Explaining Growth. A Global Research Project; Houndmills/New York: Palgrave; 159-212

Durkheim, Émile, 1893: The Division of Labor in Society; Translated by George Simpson; New York: The Free Press/London: Collier-Macmillan, 1933/1964: 40)

Elias, Norbert, 1986: Introduction [to Involvement and Detachment]; in: The Collected Works of Norbert Elias. Volume 8; edited by Stephen Quillery; Dublin: University College Dublin Press, 2003/2007

Foster, John Bellamy/McChesney, Robert W., 2009: Monopoly-Finance Capital and the Paradox of Accumulation; Monthly Review, October; http://monthlyreview.org/091001foster-mcchesney.php - 08/07/2010 6:37

Foucault, Michel, 1975: Surveiller et Punir. Naissance de la Prison; Paris: Gallimard, 1975

Foucault, Michel; 1988; The Political Technology of Individuals; Technologies of the Self; Martin, Luther H; Gutman, Huck; Hutton, Patrick H; Amherst; University of Massachusetts Press: 144-162

Fraser, Nancy/Gordon, Linda: Civil citizenship against Social Citizenship? On the Ideology of Contract-Versus-Charity; in: van Steenbergen, Bart (ed.): The Condition of Citizenship; London et altera: Sage, 1994: 90-107

Gills, Barry K./Frank, André Gunder, 1993: The Cumulation of Accumulation; in: Frank, André Gunder/Gills, Barry K., 1993: (Eds.): The World System. Five Hundred Years or Five Thousand; London/New York: Routledge: 1993: 81-114

Grinin, Leonid/Korotayev, Andrey, 2010: Will the Global Crisis Lead to Global Transformations?

Hall, Peter/Taylor, Rosemary, 1996: Political Science and the Three New Institutionalisms; in: Political Studies, 44/4: 936-958

Herrmann, Peter, 2006: Politics and Policies of the Social in the European Union – Looking at the Hidden Agendas; New York: Nova

Herrmann, Peter, 2009: Gemeinschaft der Gesellschaft – die Suche nach einem Definitionsrahmen für Prekarität; in: Hepp, Rolf (ed.): The Fragilisation of Socio-structural Components/Die Fragilisierung soziostruktureller Komponenten; Bremen: Europaeischer Hochschulverlag: 76-107

Herrmann, Peter, 2010 (Ed.): New Princedoms – Critical Remarks on Claimed Alternatives by New Life Worlds; Amsterdam: Rozenberg

Herrmann, Peter, 2010 (a): CSR – Corporate Social Responsibility versus Citizens Social Rights Or: On Regaining Political Economy; in: Herrmann, Peter, 2010 (Ed.): New Princedoms – Critical Remarks on Claimed Alternatives by New Life Worlds; Amsterdam: Rozenberg

Herrmann, Peter, 2010 (b): Prolegomena: Encore Citizenship – Revisiting or Redefining; in: Herrmann, Peter (ed.), 2010: New Princedoms – Critical Remarks on Claimed Alternatives by New Life Worlds; Amsterdam: Rozenberg

Herrmann, Peter, forthcoming (a): Searching for Global Social Policy – Economy, Economics and Governance, Amsterdam: Rozenberg

Herrmann, Peter, (b): Smart Development or Human Rights?; in: Herrmann, Peter: Rights – Developing Ownership by Linking Control over Space and Time; Bremen: Europaeischer Hochschulverlag

Herrmann, Peter/Sabine Herrenbrueck, 2007 a: Preface in: Peter Herrmann/Sabine Herrenbrueck (eds.): Changing Administration – Changing Society. Challenges for Current Social Policy; New York: Nova: vii-x

Herrmann, Peter/Sabine Herrenbrueck, 2007 b: Social Quality – Opening Individual Well-Being for a Social Perspective; in: Peter Herrmann/Sabine Herrenbrueck (eds.): Changing Administration – Changing Society. Challenges for Current Social Policy; New York: Nova: 3-22

Herrmann/Dorrity, 2009: Critique of Pure Individualism; in: Dorrity, Claire/Herrmann, Peter [eds.]: Social Professional Activity – The Search for a Minimum Common Denominator in Difference; New York: Nova Science, 2009: 1-27

History, 1010: History of technology; Wikipedia contributors; Wikipedia, The Free Encyclopedia; Date of last revision: 1 September 2010 07:55 UT; Date retrieved: 5 September 2010 07:48 UTC; Permanent link: http://en.wikipedia.org/w/index.php?title=History_of_technology&oldid=382239 313; 05/09/2010 8:51 a.m.

Horkheimer, Max, 1952: Der Begriff der Vernunft. Festrede bei der Rektoratsübergabe der Johann Wolfgang Goethe-Universität am 20. November 1951; in: Frankfurter Universitätsreden, Heft 7; Frankfurt/M.: Vittorio Klostermann: 5-17

Huffschmid, Jörg, 2009: Presentation on occasion of the Seminar Theories of Capitalism [German language], April 2009, Vienna; http://www.univie.ac.at/intpol/?p=597; 08/09/2010 2:20:02 a.m.

Hutcheson, Francis, 1738[4]: An inquiry into the original of our ideas of beauty and virtue; in two treatises. I. Concerning beauty, order, harmony, design. II. Concerning moral good and evil; London: Midwinter

Hutcheson, Francis, 1755: A System of Moral Philosophy, In Three Books. Volume I; Glasgow: Foulis/London: A Millar and T. Longman: 287 f.)

Jones Luong, Pauline/Weinthal, Erika, 1999: The NGO Paradox: Democratic Goals and Non-Democratic Outcomes in Kazakhstan; in: Europe-Asia Studies; Taylor&Francis; 51/7: 1267-1284 – www.jstor.org/stable/154122 - 05/07/2010; 00:15

Kant, Immanuel, 1784: An Answer to the Question What is Enlightenment?; http://www.english.upenn.edu/~mgamer/Etexts/kant.html - 03/10/2009 09:41

Krugman, Paul, 2009: How Did Economists Get It So Wrong; in: New York Times, September 2nd, 2009 - http://www.nytimes.com/2009/09/06/magazine/06Economic-t.html?_r=1&pagewanted=print - 03/10/2009 10:46 a.m.

Kumar, Sanjeeva, 2007: Contested Modernities in an Indigenous Domain. Community Self-Management of Forest in Post-Independence Meghalaya, a State of India; ISS Working Paper 440; Den Haag: International Institute of Social Studies at Erasmus University Rotterdam

Laskaway, Michael, 2004: Uncommitted Contemporary Work and the Search for the Self: A Qualitative Study of 28-34-Year-Old College Educated Americans; New York: New York University – PhD. Diss.

Lissakers, Karen, 1982; New York Times; July 2nd; quoted in: Magdoff, Harry/ Sweezy, Paul M., 1982

Luhmann, Niklas: 1982: Theory of Differentiation; New York: Columbia University Press

Luhmann, Niklas, 1969: Komplexität und Demokratie; in: Luhmann, Niklas: Politische Planung. Aufsätze zur Soziologie von Politik und Verwaltung; Opladen 1971: 35 ff.

Luhmann, Niklas, 1990: The Paradox of System Differentiation and the Evolution of Society; in: Alexander, Jeffrey C./Colomy, Paul (eds.): Differentiation Theory and Social Change. Comparative and Historical Perspectives; New York: Columbia University Press: 409-440

Magdoff, Harry/Sweezy, Paul M., 1982: The Deepening Crisis of U.S. Capitalism (original English-language edition, 1981; in: Monthly Review. Japanese Edition); republished under the title: Financial Instability: Where will it all End?; in: Monthly Review; April 2010; http://www.monthlyreview.org/100401magdoff-sweezy.php - 09/07/2010 10:30 a.m.

Mandeville, Bernard, 1714: The Fable of the Bees: or, Private Vices, Public Benefits. With An essay on Charity and Charity Schools, and a Search into the Nature of Society. Also, a Vindication of the Book from the Aspersions Contained in a Presentment of the Grand Jury of Middlesex, and an Abusive Letter to Lord C.; London: C. Bathurst, 1795

Marcuse, Herbert, 1964: One-Dimensional Man; Studies in the Ideology of Advanced Industrial Society; Boston: Beacon, 1964

Marx, Karl, 1875: Critique of the Gotha Programme; in: Karl Marx. Frederick Engels. Collected Works, Volume 24: Marx and Engels: 1874-83; London: Lawrence&Wishart, 1989: 75-99

Marx, Karl, 1867: Capital. A Critique of Political Economy. Volume One; http://www.marxists.org/archive/marx/works/download/pdf/Capital-Volume-I.pdf - 27/06/2011 7:15 a.m.

McMahon, Gary/Esfahani, Salehi Hadi/Squire, Lyn (eds.), 2009: Diversity in Economic Growth. Global Insights and Explanations; Cheltenham/Northampton: Edward Elgar; see also: GDN Global Development Network: Better Research, Better Policy, Better 'Developing' World – http://www.gdnet.org; 07/07/2010 6:20 a.m.

Robert Michels [Michels, Robert, 1915: Political parties: A Sociological Study of the Oligarchical Tendencies of Modern Democracy; New York: Free Press, 1966

Rügemer, Werner, 2010: Bankster vor Gericht. Kollektive Unschuld und systemische Kriminalität; in: Blätter für Deutsche und Internationale Politik, 8: 72-84

Sennett, Richard, 2006: The Culture of the New Capitalism; New Haven/London: Yale University Press

Slife, Brent F., 2004: Taking Practice Seriously: Toward a Relational Ontology; in: Journal of Theoretical and Philosophical Psychology; 24.2; 157-178

Smith, Adam, 1776: The Wealth of Nations. In two Volumes. Volume One. Introduction by Edwin R.A. Seligman; London: J.M. Dent&Sons, 1910

Soros, George, 1998: Crisis of Global Capitalism. Open Society Endangered; New York: Public Affairs

Stiglitz, Joseph, 2009: Well-being Matters in Measuring Social Progress – Invitation/program: NESC Conference: Well-Being Matters. Wednesday 7th October. Royal Hospital Kilmainham – e-mail to the author, sent by Sheila Clarke, Friday 18 September 2009 16:45

Sweeney, James, 2008: Revising Secularization Theory; in: Ward/Hoelzl [eds.], 2008: 15-29

Thatcher, Margaret, 1987: Women's Own magazine, October 31 1987 - http://briandeer.com/social/thatcher-society.htm; 27.09.09 9:21:54 a.m.

Verschraegen, Gert, 2002: Human Rights and Modern Society: A Sociological Analysis from the Perspective of Systems Theory; in: Journal of Law and Society; 29/2; Oxford: Blackwell: 258-281

Wallace, Anthony F.C., 1966: Religion: An Anthropological View; New York: Random House

Wallerstein, Immanuel, 2009: Crisis of the Capitalist System: Where Do We Go from Here?; The Harold Wolpe Lecture, University of KwaZulu-Natal, 5 November 2009; http://mrzine.monthlyreview.org/2009/wallerstein121109p.html - 09/07/2010 10:49 a.m.

Ward, Graham/Hoelzl, Michael [eds.], 2008: The New Visibility of Religion. Studies in Religion and Cultural Hermeneutics; London/New York: Continuum

Zagha, Robert/Nankani, Gobind/Gill, Indermit, 2006: Rethinking Growth; in Finance & Development; Eds.: International Monetary Fund and World Bank; 43/1: 7-11

Zinn, Karl Georg, 2010 a: Ohne Rückblick kein Durchblick – und was für ein Ausblick? Die zweite Welle der großen Krise ist noch nicht die letzte; http://www.alternative-wirtschaftspolitik.de/show/3721595.html?searchshow=zinn 08/09/2010 5:56:17 a.m.

Zinn, Karl-Georg, 2010 b: Wirtschaftskrise, das Versagen der Eliten und die Zukunft des Kapitalismus;
http://www.alternative-wirtschaftspolitik.de/show/3690935.html?searchshow =zinn 09/07/2010 10:03 a.m.

Rights-Based Approaches Against Social Injustice – Putting Social Law into Perspective

Text Prepared on Occasion of the Social Policy Conference in Cork, Ireland; September 2009

> *Men will never be free until the last king is strangled with the entrails of the last priest.*
>
> *(Diderot)*

Abstract

1) Social rights can be – and have to be – understood as a matter of thorough systematic consideration which allows to detect in social practice principles that allow defining social rights not by intuition and by referring to presumed moral laws but by systematic analysis of the way of living together.
2) In such a way the definition allows as well to develop the grammar needed to translate social rights into social law.
3) Though the contribution does not provide an immediate definition of universal social rights or a universal principle of social justice, it provides a tool for universally developing the standards needed.

The document itself approaches the issue in very fundamental terms but matters can be easily applied to contemporary social policy issues: It is not about reclaiming the rights-discourse which is currently occasionally dominated by (neo-)liberalist strategies. It is about redefining the meaning of rights-based approaches: With the renaissance and later the enlightenment the discourse had been solely based on individualist notions – defining even the concept of the social as matter of only supporting individualism and individualist self-realisation. This is as well the concept that underlies social policy development and discourse as it had been explicitly launched and institutionalised as part of and answer to industrialisation: an individualist and individualising concept of social rights. The paper argues against such approach, claiming that is needed to develop a basis that allows a truly socially determined dimension of social rights and develops from there mechanisms on the transfer of rights into law.

Prolegomena

Tony Atkinson, recently guest speaker in Cork at the Department of Applied Social Studies – giving for the time being the last presentation in the series of the William-Thompson Lectures – asked on the occasion of the Brussels Economic Forum 'In what respects are economists to blame?' and of course the concern had been the blame taken for the current crisis: a crisis of the financial markets, a recession of the productive sectors, a crisis of the social security systems and a crisis of living together. And his answer had been simple – and due to its simplicity such statement is easily pushed aside. He said:

> *I believe that economists can be rightly criticised for having become over-specialised. It is quite reasonable for the subject to be divided into micro-economics and macro-economics, but we have seen it become increasingly sub-divided and fragmented. People only study a particular form of macro-economics; they specialise in a particular approach, such as DSGE modelling. In these fields they attain high levels of technical expertise, but they are not able to react flexibly as circumstances require. Academic economists have come to resemble highly-bred race horses, trained to race on the fl at over a certain distance, but not able to jump over fences and still less to pull a plough. Economists are good in their niche, but unable to cope with a changing environment.*

(Atkinson 2009: 21)

We want to extend this by asking the question In What respects are social scientists: namely sociologists, scholars in the field of (social policy) and legal scholars to blame? Cum grano salis the same applies: overspecialisation hinders developing a broad view and a view on the fundamentals. But we want to add another dimension – which is equally valid for economics alike: Only with accepting the 'need for a broad understanding of the subject' (ibid.) we will allow ourselves as well a more radical view – and we are also forced to ask more radical questions and give more radical answers.

This implies that we will go in our presentation a path that may not be easy to follow – as long as we do not allow ourselves to leave the cage disciplinary segmentation offers.

The task seems to be a difficult one: we have to connect all dots (Ò) of the following matrix with not more than four lines in one go.

Ò	¶	Ò
¶	Ò	¶
Ò	¶	Ò

The solution is simple – just follow the numbers and do not forget to count step by step. They are in entirely different fields and still they allow drawing one line:

3	11	**10**	9
4	2	**8**	
5	7	**1**	
6			

Less metaphorically, we have to take a wider look and we have to leave the boxes in which our thinking is caught: disciplinary boundaries – or we may say as well disciplinary traps; obstacles of political censorship, be they real or anticipated; boundaries of processes – where we as academics may not allow us to coalesce with people from other ways of life in society …; speaking of 'one world', as it is today common in the area of what had been developmental aid requires as well to speak of one society, only then making the contradictions visible and subsequently allowing us to act upon them.

So join us in this undertaking of crossing borders and as well of questioning some issues we – individually or as profession – may have taken for granted without further ado.

Introduction

At the outset we find several core contradictions or at least dilemmas in policy making in the social area, some of them may serve as point of departure for the following presentation:

First, though it is very common to speak of social policy-making, this reference is hugely problematic as (i) it lacks any clear understanding of what the social actually is and (ii) it is in actually fact characterised by acting in and interacting with a vast variety of fields as the economy, the legal system, culture, the natural environment etc. (iii) It is problematic as well as the term suggests to fade out the permanently present issue of politics of social life – its definition, the negotiation of its meaning and the way of designing it.

Second, we find a second point which is commonly faded out: the difference between Sozialstaat (or Sozialer Rechtsstaat) and as well l'état providence on the one hand and the welfare state on the other hand. Hand in hand with these different concepts – underlying and resulting (or at least being maintained) – we find very different traditions in the understanding of the state (see Herrmann, 2007) and in the understanding of law. With respect to the latter it is in particular the difference between positive law and common law as dividing lines.

Third, though we find on the on hand a strong link being drawn in many debates between industrialisation and the emergence of the welfare state this stands on the other hand in contradiction (i) with the fact that the welfare state in the modern understanding is actually only very young event, being closely linked to Keynesian economics. (ii) Despite this link, we find as well a strong general claim of social policy, making reference to universal principles.

In many debates these universal principals are referring to some form of rights. As example we can mention the Universal Declaration of Human Rights and thereto-related rights-based approaches in particular in so-called development co-operation, the European Social Charter and the like. Also in academic discussions, making reference to rights-based approaches is getting increasingly common (see for instances the work led by Amartya Sen, as well the fact that this is taken up now for use in 'developed societies' – see for instance Otto/Ziegler, 2008; Otto/Ziegler, 2006:). Such reference to rights-based approaches is not only prevalent in Western Societies but also in societies in other regions of the world though we find nevertheless huge differences in its concrete form. And: we actually do not find a concrete understanding of the human rights principles which are generally suggested as universal and inalienable, indivisible, respecting inter-dependence and inter-relatedness, equality and non-discrimination, guaranteeing participation and inclusion, accountable and follow the rule of law.

Fourth, though there is more or less an agreement on certain terms – social justice, solidarity, diversity, tolerance etc. – differences and even contradictions are immediately getting obvious when it comes to the small print: what some see as emancipating and allowing people to find a place in society is by others labelled as workfare, obliging people to accept unfair conditions on the labour market and – with this: accepting loosing their rights.

Throughout all these issues there is one common moment that runs in one or another form through all these topics like a red thread. We have legal systems: lawful societies – and indeed societies full of law, where every single issue seems to be regulated by law; and at the same time these societies are in many cases apparently hugely disconnected, and in cases even undermining what we tentatively and intuitively understand as rights.

1. Individualisation of Social Rights I

Discussing citizenship and social rights refers commonly to the contemplations by Tom H. Marshall and his distinction of civil, political and social rights and his conclusion that social rights are actually the most advanced form of rights development, expressing not only a subjectively stated right on individuality and participation but going beyond such statement by setting a framework for claiming these antecedent rights and putting them into practice.

> *The civil element is composed of the rights necessary for individual freedom, liberty of the person, freedom of speech, thought and faith, the right to own property arid to conclude valid contracts, and the right to justice. The last is of a different order from the others, because it is the right to defend and assert all one's rights on terms of equality with others and by due process of law. This shows us that the institutions most directly associated with civil rights are the courts of justice. By the political element I mean the right to participate in the exercise of political power, as a member of a body invested with political authority or as an elector of the members of such a body. The corresponding institutions are parliament and councils of local government. By the social element I mean the whole range from the right to a modicum of economic welfare and security to the right to share to the full in the social heritage and to live the life of a civilised being according to the*

standards prevailing in the society. The institutions most closely connected with it are the educational system and the social services.

(Marshall, 1959: 8)

Surely, enhancing and protecting these rights is in some way indispensable. And their realisation is in particular for those indispensable who are depending on social networks which actually had been and still are being destroyed by pushing the contract culture further.

But it is success and progress by way of establishing a paradox as it is furthering itself the individualisation and meaning progress only by way of preventing the development from turning into anomic conditions. It is progress by providing a framework which allows sustaining the minimum of sociality which is necessary to maintain the individualised society. Because – contradicting Marshall's thesis of increasing socialisation – there cannot be much doubt in the character of the development that Karl Marx characterises in the following words:

> *But human beings become individuals only through the process of history. He appears originally as a species-being [Gattungswesen], clan being, herd animal -- although in no way whatever as a ζωον πολιτιχον [4] in the political sense. Exchange itself is a chief means of this individuation [Vereinzelung]. It makes the herd-like existence superfluous and dissolves it. Soon the matter [has] turned in such a way that as an individual he relates himself only to himself, while the means with which he posits himself as individual have become the making of his generality and commonness. In this community, the objective being of the individual as proprietor, say proprietor of land, is presupposed, and presupposed moreover under certain conditions which chain him to the community, or rather form a link in his chain. In bourgeois society, the worker e.g. stands there purely without objectivity, subjectively; but the thing which stands opposite him has now become the true community [Gemeinwesen], which he tries to make a meal of, and which makes a meal of him.*

(Marx, Karl: 1857/58: 420)

Or taken from Frederick Engels who forcefully states against the accusation that 'communism destroys ... individuality ... independence ... freedom'

> *The same old twaddle as we had from the true socialists and the bourgeoisie. As though there was any individuality to be destroyed in the individuals whom the division of labour has today turned against their will into cobblers, factory workers, bourgeois, lawyers, peasants, in other words, into slaves of a particular form of labour and of the*

mores, way of life, prejudices and blinkered attitudes, etc., that go with that form of labour!

(Engels, 1847: 304)

However, our thesis goes into the opposite direction, linking the analysis with general considerations on societal development. Without glorifying overcome social realities, we acknowledge the fact that development is very much characterised by the movement from status to contract, from an immediacy of social regulations by given polities to an abstract societal relationship[39] – expressively dealt with by the large philosophers and theoreticians of the state: social contract theory as for instance celebrated with the work of Jean Jacques Rousseau, notions of Treaties as promulgated by John Locke, and ideas of an Hobbesian Leviathan as quasi-voluntary subordination under an independent and nearly absolute state machinery or under a Machiavellian Prince, to be characterised as power seeking and power maintaining individual for whom the princedom plays only a secondary role.

It is important to see this not only as secular development, taking place over millennia (see for instance already Plato's works, dealing with the separation of ruler and ruled); the part that is important for us is the development in its direct intertwinement with capitalist modernisation and modernity as highly contradictory process and structure. Seen in this context, the rights-discussion is caught in the contradiction between an universalist – and idealist – strive for freedom and self-realisation of individuals and the utilitarian strive for the greatest happiness of all – actually correct would be: the 'greatest happiness for everybody and all'. In the words of Jeremy Bentham:

> *I. Nature has placed mankind under the governance of two sovereign masters, pain and pleasure. It is for them alone to point out what we ought to do, as well as to determine what we shall do. On the one hand the standard of right and wrong, on the other the chain of causes and effects, are fastened to their throne. They govern us in all we do, in all we say, in all we think: every effort we can make to throw off our subjection, will serve but to demonstrate and confirm it. In words a man may pretend to abjure their empire: but in reality he will remain subject to it all the while. The principle of utility[40] recognises this*

---

[39] though in many cases strictly hierarchical, patronising and based on arbitrary use of power

[40] Note by the Author, July 1822.
 To this denomination has of late been added, or substituted, the greatest

subjection, and assumes it for the foundation of that system, the object of which is to rear the fabric of felicity by the hands of reason and of law. Systems which attempt to question it, deal in sounds instead of sense, in caprice instead of reason, in darkness instead of light.

But enough of metaphor and declamation: it is not by such means that moral science is to be improved.

II. The principle of utility is the foundation of the present work: it will be proper therefore at the outset to give an explicit and determinate account of what is meant by it. By the principle[.] of utility is meant that principle which approves or disapproves of every action whatsoever, according to the tendency it appears to have to augment or diminish the happiness of the party whose interest is in question: or, what is the same thing in other words to promote or to oppose that happiness. I say of every action whatsoever; and therefore not only of every action of a private individual, but of every measure of government.

III. By utility is meant that property in any object, whereby it tends to produce benefit, advantage, pleasure, good, or happiness, (all this in the present case comes to the same thing) or (what comes again to the same thing) to prevent the happening of mischief, pain, evil, or unhappiness to the party whose interest is considered: if that party be the community in general, then the happiness of the community: if a particular individual, then the happiness of that individual.

(Bentham, 1789: 1 f.).

In any case, the emergence of civil rights had been very much an expression of claiming rights for enlightened individuals: as citoyen or/and bourgeois. Still, as much as it had been an expression of individualist aspirations on both sides, we have to acknowledge as well a fundamental difference – a difference which since hitherto coined the divergence of different 'social models'.

We can see this when looking at the origin of the terms citizen and citizenship which – in the words of Nancy Fraser and Linda Gordon

are powerful words. They speak of respect, of rights, of dignity. Consider the meaning and emotion packed into the French citoyen of 1789, a word that condemned tyranny and social hierarchy, while affirming self-government and status equality; that was a moment when

---

happiness or greatest felicity principle: this for shortness, instead of saying at length that principle which states the greatest happiness of all those whose interest is in question, as being the right and proper, and only right and proper and universally desirable, end of human action. ...

even women succeeded in claiming address as citoyenne rather than as madam or mademoiselle.

(Fraser/Gordon, 1994: 90)

And Ulrich K. Preuss even states that

> *I should add that originally the legal doctrine of the European continent was not rooted in utilitarianism but rather in the ethical doctrines of economic liberalism and their concept of the autonomous person. But in Germany, the industrialization process in the second half of the 19th century also entailed a change in the justification of rights according to the new requirements of industrial take-off. The right lost its ethical foundation in the moral qualification of the person and became rather a mere technical means of attributing economic goods and powers to (natural or corporate) individuals.*

(Preuss, 1986: 157 f.)

The actual role of utilitarianism as stated by Preuss may well be questioned; important is for us that he underlines as well the two strands. In any case we can see moments that are important: (i) we are concerned with orientations on individual rights and (ii) we are concerned with idealist notions of 'social rights', (α) be it as expression of the enlightened citoyen or (β) be it as moral self-obligation of the bourgeois.

Taking this as background – and thus coming back to Marshall's work – any process of Western socialisation was fundamentally characterised by strengthening individual independence, individuality and self-realisation. The state itself had been expression of this individualist approach. We can see this for instance by looking at Adam Smith who had not been opposed to every state activity but who actually wanted very much an active state as supporter, enabler of individual development, which included the states responsibility for education. On the other hand we find in the extreme case the night watch state, withdrawing from any responsibility, at most being an emergency anchor against external threats. This individualist socialisation meant as well that from now on any move towards social rights had been indeed a move towards strengthening the individuals' position against society. This can be positively seen as moving away from those 'rights' that existed in feudal societies and which Ulrich K, Preuss sees as privileges and immunities (see Preuss, 1986: 156). But of fundamental meaning is the separation of the state from the economy – or the other way round: the disembedding of the economy from general social relationships.

The market pattern, on the other hand, being related to a peculiar motive of its own, the motive of truck or barter, is capable of creating a specific institution, namely the market. Ultimately, that is why the control of the economic system by the market is of overwhelming consequence to the whole organization of society: it means no less than the running of society as an adjunct to the market. Instead of the economy being embedded in social relations, social relations are embedded in the economic system.

(Polanyi, 1944: 57)

With the question asked before this means that the new 'rights-orientation' can also be seen negatively: as development of an anonymous state which dissolved the immediate social control by an abstract system of regulations, primarily oriented on positions of individuals in society, but barely on measures of socialisation; an important, though double-edged – exception is the area of education. This contradicts strongly for instance the position taken by François Ewald who claims

The very name given to it – 'Welfare State' – suffices to show that as yet it has scarcely been considered in its positive aspects[41]. It denotes a State that, while no longer analysable in terms of the liberal model, is not seen as being in transition to a future socialist state either.

This hypothesis suggests a thorough reconsideration of the perspective from which both the institutions and the practices that characterise this new positive entity should be looked at. They ought no longer to be analysed as a mere set of measures aimed at correcting the harshness and injustices of a liberal State, but as the coordinates of a new type of political space with an internal logic of its own.

(Ewald, 1986: 40)

Sure, these protective and supportive measures had been indispensable and extremely valuable for the members of the working class and even more so for those who had been excluded even from that position of dependence. But at the same time it can be shown that everything was about protecting the polity – the state of the ruling classes – against the 'outcasts': integration as keyword meant subordination under the conditions of the class society: be it by direct inclusion into the capitalist system of exploitation or be it by indirect inclusion via the workhouses

---

[41] [Footnote in cited text:] The term 'État-providence [Welfare State]' was the one used by liberals in the nineteenth century to deride the social reformers' projects.

(see Powell, 1992). In this light surely the state of the poor laws but also the later welfare states as they arose as appendix to the Keynesian economic strategy had been 'states' rather than 'a new type of political space'; and if they really had not only been 'set of measures aimed at correcting the harshness and injustices of a liberal State', they had been much less: a means of keeping a very specific accumulation regime functioning and a means of specifically undermining what they claimed to enhance: the social individual. The fact that decommodification does not question the functional principles of capitalist market society means as well that social policy as policy of decommodification basically only sustains the reduction of human existence on the existence of individuals – before we quoted Marx' Grundrisse on this. And here we can say that decommodification depends as much on the capitalist commodification as the devil, by claiming to be anti-christ, is in actual fact manifesting the own dependency on Christianity. Required for a sound development of rights-based policies is a more fundamental turn than a simple internal negation. In the words of Karl Marx:

> *The standpoint of the old materialism is civil society; the standpoint of the new is human society, or social humanity.*

(Marx, 1845: 5)

2. Excursus – Sozialstaat and Welfare State

This becomes also clear when we look at the heavy load of the debate on the welfare state – and its predecessor: the German 'Sozialstaat' (or 'Soziale Rechtsstaat') (see Preuss, 1986). The German concept (very much like its French complement: 'l'état providence') is going back to Lorenz von Stein and the question of integrating the industrial proletariat. His approach rested on three pillars, namely (i) social provisions, (ii) social democracy (in German: Soziale Demokratie which is not the same as Sozialdemokratie [both translating into social democracy]; (iii) freedom of assembly as means of personal self-determination and self-assertion against state and economy (see in this context as well Koslowski, 1989).

Later, Hermann Heller explicitly positioned this concept against liberal capitalism and also against socialism. Ulrich K. Preuss points out that welfare state, however, is a concept that is less a political concept but closely linked to the political economy of John Maynard Keynes who sees welfare policy as matter of securing the economic development. He *stated the 'psychological law' that the increase of income would increase the consumption ... After World War II all advanced capitalist societies established some sort of Welfare State on the basis of Keynes' economic theory and thus institutionalized the dynamic of increasing mass spending power and consumption.*

(Preuss, op.cit.: 153)

From here it is indeed easy to state that

[t]he differences in the theoretical fundaments of Heller's concept of the 'Sozialer Rechtsstaat' and the 'Keynesian Welfare State' are clear. Heller's idea is based on a socio-political theory with strong ethical notions to overcome capitalism and to emancipate the proletariat, whereas the Keynesian Welfare State is the application of an economic theory for the sake of unfaltering the potential of capitalism under critical conditions – and fortunately this entailed the protection and permanent increase of mass income.

(ibid.: 153 f.)

The paradox is that debate on welfare retrenchment as it is commonly put forward needs careful consideration:

First, empirically the retrenchment as matter of reduction of resources is by no means the central problem – in actual fact the spending for social policy relevant matters cannot necessarily be validated by empirical data. More problematic is the change of the underlying concept of social challenges. For instance, poverty and social disparities are by proponents of the new system less a problem than deactivation and reliance on transfers.

Second, to use the words of François Ewald as quoted above (see Ewald, 1986: 40) the welfare state has indeed its own logic. But this logic is derived from the functioning of the economy rather than an understanding of peoples' needs and the understanding of a social system. And it is fundamentally individualist.

Third, the malfunctions of the current welfare state – and such statement cannot claim any originality – are in actual fact a lack of implementing the very principles of Keynesian policies. However, stating this means to acknowledge (i) that social policy in this vein is an appendix to capitalism and (ii) that as such (α) it is based on principally individualised relationships – the contract-basis of capitalist systems, as it will be explored in the following section – and (β) it lacks any consideration of needs and principles of social rights.

And going even a step further, it can then be asked if and to which extent the Keynesian welfare state is fundamentally different from other capitalist concepts as far as the political economy of social law is concerned. Finally it had been the conservative Carl Schmitt who claimed that it would be liberalism that aims on solving the social question by increasing production and stimulating consumption (cf. Schmitt, 1958: 489)

3. Individualisation of Social Rights II

At the extreme end we find two legally central features that are in one or another for characterising social policies today. The one is the pseudo-solidaristic principle of the German social insurance system; the other is the pseudo-neutral principle of contracts. As the latter is in practice, in terms of its functional principle, also underlying the social insurance systems, it may briefly be characterised by its elements – a secularised holy trinity of provision, provider and consumer/user. A contract then is triangular relationship between provision/service – provider – user or customer, where the contractual conditions are based on free will between formally equal parties, with mutual obligations and benefits and being limited to the explicit contractual agreement. Here we find as well a fundamental difference in comparison with rights: the latter are not characterised by counter-rights.

Following from here, the current use of the concept of social rights is always caught in the individualist cage of claimants rather than opening into a wider understanding of general mutuality.

The Social Remainder

Of course, all this does not mean that the social is entirely destructed, it only means that it is annexed – from the beginning of being treated as The Theory of Moral Sentiments by Adam Smith (Smith, 1759:), it is now established as policy of flanking economic processes. Importantly, the economic and soci(et)al processes are themselves split (i) from each other and (ii) in themselves. The state – as 'total ideal capitalist' (Lenin) – is positioned outside and at the very same time inside of the economic process.

Allocation was the inherent, apolitical and neutral principle of the market and its efficiency, whereas distribution was a political principle of justice.

(Preuss, op. cit.: 157)

This has far reaching consequences if it comes to the definition of social rights as they are now explicitly set apart from economic relations although they are implicitly part of the overall process. The problem in question is that allocation as economic process establishes – de facto – inequalities. Even a radical defender of the market economy as Mario Monti, former European Commissioner ascertains

My starting point is the following: if the world economy is in crisis, the market economy is even more in crisis.

It is seen as unfair, having generated unacceptable inequalities, and inefficient, having attracted massive resources into financial activities whose contribution to the economy is questioned. Yet the world needs an integrated market economy which is a necessary, though by no means sufficient condition for growth and welfare. The key test for market economies, and perhaps even for democracies, in my view, will be whether they master the growing inequalities, including within countries, caused by ungoverned globalisation and aggravated by the crisis.

(Monti, 2009: 8 f.)

And as much as the market – and subsequent social inequality – is an economic fact, here indirectly admitted by Monti, as much is distribution part of the economic process. But it is artificially externalised and left to political intervention. And more importantly vice versa, allocation by the market is itself explicitly left outside of political control, suggested to be neutral. In other words, we have an inverse relationship of (the reach of) socialisation. However, this is in actual fact a 'soci(et)al impossibility'. To use the words of Karl Polanyi:

A self-regulating market demands nothing less than the institutional separation of society into an economic and political sphere. Such a dichotomy is, in effect, merely the restatement, from the point of view of society as a whole, of the existence of a self-regulating market. It might be argued that the separateness of the two spheres obtains in every type of society at all times. Such an interference, however, would be based on a fallacy. True, no society can exist without a system of some kind which ensures order in the production and distribution of goods. But that does not imply the existence of separate economic institutions; normally, the economic order is merely a function of the social, in which it is contained. Neither under tribal, nor feudal, nor mercantile conditions was there ... a separate economic system in society. Nineteenth century society, in which economic activity was isolated and imputed to a distinctive economic motive, was, indeed, a singular departure.

(Polanyi, op.cit.: 71)

And we can add another step: With this separation we find also the separation of the individual from society in form of a suggested confrontation of state and civil society.

Law – Its General Development and its Relevance for the Social

To emphasise again, the relationship between rights and law stands at the core of our presentation. According to Ernest Joseph Weinrib, Immanuel Kant maintains a unity of the reasoning and free individual and law:

Ascribing to legality an inherent normative nature arises from Kant's account of free choice. Legality as an idea of reason is 'practical' in Kant's sense of being grounded in the notion of purposeful activity. As the determining ground of free choice, practical reason provides norms. However, practical reason does not impose any demands on free choice from without; in merely makes explicit the normativeness implicit in purposivness as a spontaneous causality of concepts. The meaning of normativeness is precisely the determination of free choice in accordance with in accordance with its own nature.

(Weinrib, 1995: 93)

This includes, of course, especially in the Kantian tradition the orientation on practice. Having said this, we have to recognise as well that this orientation on practice is very much rooted in an idealist understanding of practice as universalist principle with its orientation on will as guideline. Apart from freedom and the strive for happiness,[42] which is dominant in Kant's thinking, this principal orientation on practical reason is opening a trap, namely the need to delink positive law from moral understanding. In Immanuel Kant's own words we learn that

---

[42] Though in a distinct understanding if compared with that of Bentham.

[i]f a rational being is to think of his maxims as practical universal laws, he can think of them only as principles that contain the determining ground of the will not by their matter but only by their form.

(Kant, 1788: 24)

In general terms, law can then be seen as a 'principle of order' (Jenkins, Iredell: Social Order and the Limits of Law. A Theoretical Essay; Princeton: Princeton University Press 1980: 69) which maintains two interconnected dimensions: relations and processes.

We have to point on different dimensions of the definition of law:

First, law is generally seen as 'negative': a means of punishment, restoring order or maintaining a given order where it is in danger of breaking up *(see for instance Gramsci, 1957/1978: 187)*

Second, at the same time the origin of law is empirically grounded in positive norms. Iredell Jenkins distinguishes between

three fundamental modes of law: expository, prescriptive, and normative.

(Jenkins, 1980: 69)

This corresponds with what Jenkins calls an actual order, an ideal order and an open provisional order (cf. ibid.: 96) which he sees as well maintained as a kind of – to use our terms – holy trinity underlying the concept of positive law.

Search for the Ideal Order

Third, the actual question is from where do we get the 'ideal order' that is underlying the process of defining – social – law. We can find two points of reference that are seemingly independent from each other. The one that usually springs first to mind – especially when it comes to social law – is the reference to general values. Though they provide a general point of reference, they are equally generally blurred. Moreover, looking at the derivation of such values we see various patterns, in particular lex aeterna, jus divinum and lex naturalis. Thomas Aquinas contemplates on divine law and human law in the following words.

Respondo dicendum quoe, sicut supradicium est, lex est quoddam dictamen practicae rationis. Similis autem processus esse invenitur rationis principiis ad quasdam conclusions procedit, ut superius habitum est. Secundo hoc ergo dicendum est quod, sicut in ratione speculative ex principiis indemonstrabilibus naturaliter cognitis procuntur conclusions diversarum scientiarum, quarum cognito non est nobis naturaliter indita, sed per industriam ratinonis inventa; it etiam ex praececommunibus et indemonstrabilibus, necesse est quod ratio humana procedfat ad aliqua magis particulariter disponenda. Et istae particulares dispositionnes adinvetnaet secundum rationem humanam, dicuntur leges humanae, servatis aliis conditionibus quae pertinent ad ratinem legis, ut supra dictum est. Unde Tullius dicit in sua Rhetor, quod initium iuris est natura profectum; deinde queadam in consuetudinem ex utilitate rationis venerunt; postea res et natura profectum; deinde quaedam in consuetudinem ex utilitate rationis venerunt; postea res et a natura profectas at a consuetudine probatas legum metus et religio sanxit.

(Aquinatis, 1265-1273: 415)

Oliver Wendell Holmes – being concerned with common law – makes a similar point, at least avoiding to provide practical criteria and even more than Aquinas avoiding to establish a firm link to societal practice. He says that

[t]he remoter and more general aspects of the law are those which give it universal interest. It is through them that you not only become a great master in your calling, but connect your subject with the universe and catch an echo of the infinite, a glimpse of its unfathomable process, a hint of the universal law.

(Holmes, 1896: 1030)

And looking at today's legislative systems, we can get the impression of rights being void of any origin in wider practice, instead being seen as autopietic system. To borrow the words of Niklas Luhmann:

Man gelangt auf diese Weise zu einem theoretisch systematisierten, auf Regeln und Prinzipien gebrachten positiven Recht – und kann damit zufrieden sein. Die traditionelle Frage nach der Gerechtigkeit des Rechts verliert so jede praktische Bedeutung. Sie kann weder als dritter Weg neben Recht und Unrecht hinzugefügt werden, noch bezeichnet sie eines der Programme des Systems – so also ob es neben dem Baurecht, und dem Straßenverkehrsrecht, dem Erbrecht und dem Urheberrecht noch gerechtes Recht gäbe. Die Konsequenz ist: daß man Fragen der Gerechtigkeit des Rechts nur noch als Fragen der Begründung des Rechts im Medium der Moral; und daß man dann mit groeßter Muehe nach einem Platz für die Ethik im Recht Ausschau haelt. Oder daß man Gerechtigkeit für ein gesamtgesellschaftliches Prinzip haelt, das für alle Lebensbereiche gilt und im Recht nur eine besondere Form annimmt.

(Luhmann, 1993: 216)

In summa, with or without affirmation the legislative system is detached from the actual human social practice.

However, this overlooks the other source already entailed in what Aquinas nevertheless implied. It is human practice that is at the origin, we can say more precisely: it is the rectified or contradictory interaction between people and the interaction of people with their natural and institutional environment. C.W. Maris and F.C.L.M Jacobs see social practice (closely understood as interactive practice of 'productive interaction') as process that is immediately connected with processes of inter-subjective generation of moral standards and vice versa: the inter-subjective generation of moral standards as means that guides practice:

> *Historisch gezien bestaat er ongetwijfeld een nauw feitelijk verband tussen recht en moraal. In de oorsprong van de menselijke geschiedenis leeft men in kleine en weinig veranderlijke groepen, meestal en uitgebreide familie onder leiding van de oudere mannen. ... In zo'n samenleving vormt het recht één ongedifferentieerd geheel met de overgeleverde moraal e religie.*[43]

(Maris/Jacobs, 1997: 5)

Later, Jeremy Bentham brought this forward, clearly referring to a very specific practice, stating:

> *In the foregoing chapter it has been shown at large that goodness or badness cannot, with any propriety, be predicated of motives. Is there nothing then about a man that can properly be termed good or bad, when, on such or such an occasion, he suffers himself to be governed by such or such a motive? Yes, certainly: his disposition. Now disposition is a kind of fictitious entity, feigned for the convenience of discourse, in order to express what there is supposed to be permanent in a man's frame of mind, where, on such or such an occasion, he has been influenced by sued or such a motive, to engage in an act, which, as it appeared to him, was of such or such a tendency.*
>
> *II. It is with disposition as with every thing else: it will be good or bad according to its effects: according to the effects it has in augmenting or*

---

[43] It seems to be characteristic that we find such a frank statement in the Dutch literature, even in terms of such analysis reflecting the pragmatic tradition, heavily influenced by Calvinist thinking.

diminishing the happiness of the community. A man's disposition may accordingly be considered in two points of view: according to the influence it has, either, 1. on his own happiness: or, 2. on the happiness of others. Viewed in both these lights together, or in either of them indiscriminately, it may be termed, on the one hand, good; on the other, bad; or, in flagrant cases, depraved.

(Bentham, 1789: 131).

In other words, it is the presumed utilitarian character of human action that is considered as replacing any kind of values that would be needed to be set from outside.

Karl Marx, on the other hand, opposes such generalising approach towards human action and the respective motivation, considering the underlying class structure as fundamentally determining the different definitions of lawfulness. We read

And does not this crude view, which lays down a common definition for different kinds of action and leaves the difference out of account, itself bring about its own destruction? If every violation of property without distinction, without a more exact definition, is termed theft, will not all private property be theft? By my private ownership do I not exclude every other person from this ownership? Do I not thereby violate his right of ownership? If you deny the difference between essentially different kinds of the same crime, you are denying that crime itself is different from right, you are abolishing right itself, for every crime has an aspect in common with right. Hence it is a fact, attested equally by history and reason, that undifferentiated severity makes punishment wholly unsuccessful, for it does away with punishment as a success for right.

(Marx, 1842: 228)

And he continues

The definite content of a violation of the law is the limit of a definite crime. The measure of this content is therefore the measure of the crime. In the case of property this measure is its value. Whereas personality, whatever its limits, is always a whole, property always exists only within a definite limit that is not only determinable but determined, not only measurable but measured. Value is the civil mode of existence of property, the logical expression through which it first becomes socially comprehensible and communicable.

(ibid.: 229)

This culminates in stating the conviction that

> *[t]he sole equality to be found in the actual life of animals is the equality between one animal and other animals of the same species; it is the equality of the given species with itself, but not the equality of the genus.*

(ibid.: 30)

In other words, we can see that at least the law in the modern capitalist society is getting independent from social and societal practice and gaining meaning solely in self-referential dimensions – from a Marxist standpoint reflecting the class society, in the Kantian perspective the 'determining ground of the will not by their matter but only by their form.' Niklas Luhmann, for instance, interprets it then later as matter of autopoietic systems which communicate by binary codes of general media. In his work on The Law of Society we read

> *Die Einheit des Rechtssystems ist im Rechtssystem zunaechst in der Form der operativen Sequenzen gegeben, die das System autopoietisch reproduzieren. Die Operationen koennen ihre Systemzugehoerigkeit beobachten, also System und Umwelt unterscheiden. Das Unterscheiden aktualisiert Selbstreferenz, also eine Bezeichnung des sich bezeichnenden Systems im Unterschied zu allem anderen.*

(Luhmann, 1993: 214)

Looking at the historical development and drawing on the work by Yitzhak Berman and Peter Herrmann we arrive at the following picture that is relevant for analysing social rights and their translation into social law.

APPROACH TO REALITY	APPROACH TO LAW
Immediate appropriation of nature	Spontaneous natural law – as law of nature ('environmental law')
Successive division of labour	Divine law
Successive division of control	Canon law[44]
Emergence of systems of communal production[45]	Common law
Heavily exchange based economies and societies emphasising the importance of 'civic-ness' as distinct area	Beginning with the Lex Duodecim Tabularum of Roman law and the later civil law
Prospected social quality society	Global Human Rights Approach

(From: Berman/Herrmann, 2012:35)

Figure 5

Underlying is a definition of 'the social' as the outcome of the interaction between people (constituted as actors) and their constructed and natural environment. With this in mind its subject matter refers to people's productive and reproductive relationships. In other words

- the constitutive interdependency between processes of self-realisation and processes of the formation of collective identities
- is a condition for 'the social', realised by the interactions of
  o actors, being – with their self-referential capacity – competent to act
  o and their framing structure, which translates immediately into the context of human relationships.

We then can strive for a new definition of social law – and dispose as well of a tool for assessing existing social law. We arrive at it by turning away from idealist, intuitive, and at the end very shallow, relative normative notions of social rights and social justice (be they based on anthropological concepts of nature and natural being or be they based on any kind of divinity) and by turning towards an understanding that is based on determining human practice and the inherent power relationships. This goes beyond John Rawls and Ronald Dworkins approach, described by the latter in the following:

---

[44] Though in a wider understanding, as law of religious bodies/institutions
[45] However, this goes well hand in hand with a separation of power and control, thus including feudal and especially capitalist systems

It is the task of moral philosophy, according to the technique of equilibrium, to provide a structure of principle that supports these immediate convictions about which we are more or less secure, with two goals in mind. First, this structure of principles must explain the convictions by showing the underlying assumptions they reflect; second it must provide guidance in those cases about which we have either no convictions or weak or contradictory convictions. If we are unsure, for example, whether economic institutions that allow great disparity of wealth are unjust, we may turn to the principles that explain our confident convictions, and then apply these principles to that difficult issue.

But the process is not simply one of finding principles that accommodate our more-or-less settled judgement. These principles must support, and not merely account for, our judgements, and this means that the principles must have independent appeal to our moral sense.

(Dworkin, 1978²: 155)

We propose, however, to go beyond moral principles and look for principles that can be derived from real acting people rather than from idealised – and idealist – moral norms. A preliminary proposal can be taken from Peter Herrmann and Claire Dorrity who suggest the following points of reference:

- appropriateness as
  - o 'availing of property'[46] and
  - o adequacy and
- equality as
  - o contestable legitimacy ('control of the system') and
  - o empowerment in terms of developing capabilities ('control of the own life and development')

---

[46] Not to be confused with property formation under private law.

The tensions and options are as follows:

		appropriation	
		property	adequacy
equality	legitimacy		
	empowerment		

(from Herrmann/Dorrity, 2009: 14)

Figure 6

Now the solution is quite simple: we propose to start from concrete human practice in order to find – according to the reference points of appropriation and equality standards – and with this demands – for social law. Going hand in hand with the two reference points are two dimensions of power, namely (i) power with the orientation on pouvoir, i.e. abilities and (ii) power with the link to possere, i.e. the realm of possibilities, of 'what can be'.
Third, we can then say that

> *[p]ositive law assumes an ordered social context that exhibits certain deficiencies: it envisages more desirable – an ideal – ordering of the context; it prescribes the steps to be taken in order to move the actual towards the ideal; and it orders that these measures be instituted. That is, positive law is at once expository, normative prescriptive, advisory, and imperative. But it is positive law as a means to an end ...*

(Jenkins, 1980: 75)

But it is exactly here where the question arises: How can we determine the grammar for translating rights into law.

Ernst Bloch makes us aware of four different kinds of possibilities, namely (i) the formally possible – what is possible according to its logical structure; (ii) the objectively possible – possible being based on assumptions on the ground of epistemologically based knowledge; (iii) the objectively possible – possible as it follows from the options inherently given by the object; (iv) and the objectively real possible – possible by following the latency and tendency which is inherent in its elementary form (see Bloch, 1959: 258-288; cf. Herrmann, forthcoming)

We can link this to what we know from Karl Marx' economic analysis with respect to the analytical division of the economic process, the dimensions being production, consumption, distribution and exchange (see Marx, 1857-58: in particular the introduction; cf. Herrmann, forthcoming) and arrive at the following combination – the first column proposing a horizon of possibilities, referring to Ernst Bloch, the second referring to the analytical differentiation of the economic process as outlined by Karl Marx.[47]

HORIZON OF POSSIBILITIES	ECONOMIC PROCESS
formally possible – according to its logical structure	*exchange*
objectively possible – based on assumptions on the ground of epistemologically based knowledge	*distribution*
objectively possible – following the options inherently given by the object	*consumption*
objectively real possible – following the latency and tendency which is inherent in its elementary form	*production*

Figure 7

So far this seems to be an academic exercise. But how does it link to the age-old question of how to bring approaches of positive law on the one hand and subjective rights approaches together (see on this question for instance Hart, 1976:; Dworkin, 1978[2]). The proposal we want to make in order to arrive at least at a pathway that allows a proper analytical framework for systematically elaborating rights goes back to the emergence of rights from practice. This means to bring the development of rights back to what is really possible –and returning with this to the centrality of the sphere of production for determining rights. Production is, here, understood as the entirety of producing the social: social relationships, their relation to the natural and institutional environment. The need to define and secure rights evolves from the conflicts within this process of production. In order of doing

---

[47] This and the following figures have to be read bottom-up.

so we have to look for a non-affirmative role, that employs two levels:
(i) the existing society, i.e. mode of production; (ii) the perspective on
changing societies. In both regards we have to think about complex
fields as they are outlined in (from Herrmann/Dorrity, 2009: 14)

Figure 6. We can then in a relatively simple process move between norm-defining and norm-applying dimensions of the legal process as they are briefly outlined in the following (with some reference to Iredell Jenkins (see Jenkins, op.cit.):

HORIZON OF POSSIBILITIES	ECONOMIC PROCESS	LEGAL PERSPECTIVE
formally possible – according to its logical structure	*exchange*	*contract law* – not least as matter of correctly implementing legal mechanisms, including assessment and monitoring of legal procedures
objectively possible – based on assumptions on the ground of epistemologically based knowledge	*distribution*	*expository law* - traditional social law as securing a temporary social balance and compensation for inequalities
objectively possible – following the options inherently given by the object	*consumption*	*prescriptive law* – utilising existing resources for enhancing critical positions
objectively real possible – following the latency and tendency which is inherent in its elementary form	*production*	*normative law* – derivation of social norms by starting from defining the productive process as production of the social; distinctively as non-affirmative orientation as far as power imbalances and contradictions are concerned

Figure 8

Indeed, the major difference is that we bring the definition of rights – and subsequently law – back to the origins and put the discussion back on its feet. Actually we can make another step forward, adding some examples for criteria of social law in connection with what had been outlined in the previous synopsis. Methodologically a crucial point is to go systematically through the different steps of looking at the options given in the respective dimension of the productive process.[48] Not less important is to keep in mind that that standard for setting standards are appropriateness and equality – the latter not as moral, intuitive instance but as matter of logic: a rule of non-equality[49] would necessarily evoke situations of rights that are mutually excluding. The actual problem with this is twofold. First it is about individual injustice: rights on the expense of somebody else logically means the disrespect of the rights of the other. Second, more importantly in our context: such rights are by definition not social rights because they are dealing with the situation of individuals. To turn it around: social rights have to start by defining the social situation and the terms by which it allows people to develop – and importantly it is about individuals developing by existing with others.[50]

---

[48] It seems to me more opportune to speak of a productive process rather then simply an economic process – such terminological shift underlines the social dimension and the integrated character of what is usually termed economic process.

[49] Which does mean inequality as the latter may be necessary to obtain equality as the debate on equal opportunities shows.

[50] For further elaboration see the Social Quality debate and not least the debates on Social Quality and its relation to Human Development, Capability Approach etc. – for instance in Gaspers, et altera 2008; Herrmann2009: 133-188

HORIZON OF POSSIBILITIES	ECONOMIC PROCESS	LEGAL PERSPECTIVE	FOCUS OF DEFINING SOCIAL RIGHTS
formally possible – according to its logical structure	*exchange*	*contract law* – not least as matter of correctly implementing legal mechanisms, including assessment and monitoring of legal procedures	*administrative level – defining accountability and transparency of social law implementation based on coordinated procedures; right to have an account*
objectively possible – based on assumptions on the ground of epistemologically based knowledge	*distribution*	*expository law* - traditional social law as securing a temporary social balance and compensation for inequalities	*social transfers – moving to an unconditional basic income*
objectively possible – following the options inherently given by the object	*consumption*	*prescriptive law* – utilising existing resources for enhancing critical positions	*societal positioning* – allowing people to find social and societal positions that facilitate their active contribution to societal development; enhancing the scope of independence in which people can act in society
objectively real possible – following the latency and tendency which is inherent in its elementary form	*production*	*normative law* – derivation of social norms by starting from defining the productive process as production of the social; distinctively as non-affirmative orientation as far as power imbalances and contradictions are concerned	*working conditions* – being concerned with conditions under which employment takes place and the range of socially valued activities. Not least utilising production as means allowing people to develop their personalities rather than only applying skills

Figure 9

Let us attempt to give in a final step concrete examples for social rights – taking areas that are typically seen as problematic when it comes to discussing social rights. These will be only presented to point out some issues of relevance, being left for further discussion elsewhere.

HORIZON OF POSSIBILITIES	ECONOMIC PROCESS	LEGAL PERSPECTIVE	FOCUS OF DEFINING SOCIAL RIGHTS	SOCIAL LAW
formally possible – according to its logical structure	*exchange*	*contract law –* not least as matter of correctly implementing legal mechanisms, including assessment and monitoring of legal procedures	*administrative level – defining accountability and transparency of social law*	implementation based on coordinated procedures; right to have an account
objectively possible – based on assumptions on the ground of epistemologically based knowledge	*distribution*	*expository law -* traditional social law as securing a temporary social balance and compensation for inequalities	*social transfers – moving to an unconditional basic income*	individualised transfers for instance of child benefits that does not allow a parent to make use for non-child related matters
objectively possible – following the options inherently given by the object	*consumption*	*prescriptive law – utilising*	*societal positioning –* allowing people to find social and societal positions that facilitate their active contribution to societal development	right to training and education[51]
objectively real possible – following the latency and tendency which is inherent in its elementary form	*production*	*normative law –* derivation of social norms by starting from defining the productive process as production of the social; distinctively as non-affirmative orientation as far as power imbalances and contradictions are concerned	*working conditions –* being concerned with conditions under which employment takes place and the range of socially valued activities. Not least utilising production as means allowing people to develop their personalities rather than only applying skills – decommodification of production	recognition of the value of women's work as matter of respecting eligibility to services etc. ('individualisation of rights')

Figure 10

51   Boccara, 2002

Epilogue – Seven Theses

This is an ambitious approach, though at the end it is very simple – not least when we discuss it in concreto.

1) Again, it is decisive to critically discuss Marshall's understanding of citizenship as process of increasing socialisation. Socialisation, as we find it within capitalism, is fundamentally an individualising process. As important social justice is in terms within this system, they remain very much de-emancipating. (i) In regard to the political economy of the welfare state, a fundamental problem is its privatist structure as it is systematically build into the structure of the contractualisation of socio-economic relationship. (ii) In respect to political structures the fundamental problem is the separation of the economic and political system, culminating in the confrontation of bourgeois and citoyen or in other terms corporations and civil society organisations. So we arrive even at a tripartite division as the state as political entity is not only – artificially and seemingly – separated from the economic sphere but as well from the presumed civil sphere. This is frankly stated by Lorenz von Stein when he says:

> *Das Wesen der Regierung ist die Vollziehung des Gesetzes durch ihre einheitliche persönliche Gewalt. In der Regierung erscheint der Staat als selbstthätige, und daher nothwendig einheitlich einheitliche organisirte Persönlichkeit. Der Begriff der einheitlichen That schließt die freie Teilnahme des Einzelnen aus; es ist keine That möglich, wenn sie nicht als persönliche Einheit auftritt. Die Regierung ist verantwortlich, aber sie ist weder frei noch unfrei, sondern sie ist ein persönlicher Organismus.*

(von Stein, 1869^2: 6)

2) We see today an alarming orientation towards a suggested increase of civil society. Though this is surely a multifarious topic, on important point with this development is a return to earlier soci(et)al patterns of social organisations – emphasising civil rights means that we are again required to look for means to live them; and rather than seeing it as an increasing awareness of the importance of societal movements we can see such development as well as expression of a development that undermines even the fundamentals of so-called modern societies.

3) In actual fact we can see such developments not least in the economic sphere: the popular and papal lament about greed as important explanans of the current crisis, the tendency towards a renaissance of Keynesianism but also the various alternative movements as for instance the search for

alternative lifestyles, the reminiscence on household economies and direct exchange are – to say the least – problematic and limited. Leaving the diversity of issues out of consideration, one of the principal problems is that they are at most based in subjectivist approaches towards social justice. A society can only be as smart as the economic conditions are – the question of hegemony has to follow the fundamental structures in order to intervene rather than attempting to act from outside.

4) We then need a fundamental shift that understands the fundamentally social character of economic relations and processes and vice versa the fundamentally economic character of social relations and processes. This has to go far beyond the debates on 'competitiveness of welfare models' and the calculations on the 'Costs of Non-social Policy' (see Fouarge, 2003:). And it has to go further than asking the question 'Can the Welfare State Compete?' (see e.g. Pfaller/Gough/Therborn, Göran [eds.], 1991).

5) Social law has to start from here and look for ways of remerging allocation and distribution as two sides of the very same process. It is in this way that we can arrive at a strategy of social policy which is guided by looking for far-reaching alternative. It is the way to which we can open the door with a final quote from Karl Marx – already cited before

> The standpoint of the old materialism is civil society; the standpoint of the new is human society, or social humanity.
>
> (Marx, 1845: 5)

This is the core of current renaissances of values, the rejection of greed – supposedly so important in the current crisis. It is not about values but about the reestablishment of the social as basis of living together. Again the words of Karl Polanyi:

> After a century of blind 'improvement' man is restoring his 'habitation'. If industrialism is not to extinguish the race, it must be subordinated to the requirements of man's nature. The true criticism of market society is not that it is based on economics – in a sense every society must be based on it – but that its economy was based on self-interest. Such an organization of economic life is entirely unnatural, in the strictly empirical sense of exceptional.
>
> (Polanyi, op.cit.: 249)

The individualism and greed is nothing else than individuals' forced and alienated attempt to follow the pathway of a dehumanised society where rights are dissolved into individual claims.

6) Though there is a good reason to analytically distinguish between different dimensions as social rights, social provisions, social security, perhaps even between needs and wants it is at the end crucial to think them together, thus allowing as well to develop an approach that is suitable for the one world we are living in rather than distinguishing between the debate on social rights for the so-called developing world and the debate on the right to social protection for the so-called developed world.

7) If we are not ready for such a fundamental shift, and remain stuck in demanding rights for individuals we are well be overrun by a new prince: individualist, the social reduced on self-fulfilment, on greatest happiness and living in the illusion of a Robinsonade in Wealth and forcefully guided by a new Prince.

References

Aquinatis, S. Thomae, 1265-1273: Summa Theologiae; Taurioni/Romae: Marietti, 1952

Atkinson, Anthony B.: Three questions about the global economic crisis and three conclusions for EU and Member State policy-makers; in: European Commission. Directorate General for Economic and Financial Affairs (Ed.): Beyond the Crisis: A Changing Economic Landscape. Keynote Speeches at the Brussels Economic Forum 2009; ECFIN Economic Brief; 2. June 2009: 21-324

Bentham Bentham, Jeremy, 1789: An Introduction to the Principles of Morals and Legislation. With an Introduction by Laurene J Flaneur; New York: Hafner1948

Berman, Yitzhak/Herrmann, Peter, 2012: Systems of Law and Social Quality; in: Social & Public Policy Review; Social & Public Policy Review, 2012; 6, 1, pp. 20-39 http://www.uppress.co.uk/socialpolicy_pdf/Berman%20herman.pdf

Bloch, Ernst, 1959: Prinzip Hoffnung; Frankfurt/M: Suhrkamp [written in 1938-1947; reviewed 1953 and 1959]

Boccara, Paul, 2002: Pour une Sécurité d'emploi ou de formation en Europe; Pantin: Espere/Le Temps des Cersies

Dworkin, Ronald M., 1978[2]: Taking Rights Seriously; Cambridge/Mass.: Harvard University Press:

Dworkin, Ronald M., 1978[2]: Taking Rights Seriously; Cambridge/Mass.: Harvard University Press

Engels, Frederick, 1847: The Communists and Karl Heinzen. Second Article. Deutsche-Brüsseler-Zeitung No. 80, October 7, 1847; in: Karl Marx. Frederick Engels. Collected Works. Volume 6: Marx and Engels: 1845-1848; London: Lawrence&Wishart, 1976; 298-306

Ewald, François: A Concept of Social Law; in: Teubner, Gunter (ed.), 1986: Dilemmas of Law in the Welfare State; Berlin/New York: Walter de Gruyter, 1986: 40-75

Fouarge, Didier, 2003: Costs of Non-Social Policy: Towards an Economic Framework of Quality Social Policies and the Costs of Not Having Them; Ed.: European Commission. DG of Employment and Social Affairs; http://www.ucc.ie/social_policy/EU-docs-socpol/Fouarge_costofnonsoc_final_en.pdf - 27/07/2009 12:00 p.m.

Fraser, Nancy/Gordon, Linda: Civil citizenship against Social Citizenship? On the Ideology of Contract-Versus-Charity; in: van Steenbergen, Bart (ed.): The Condition of Citizenship; London et altera: Sage, 1994: 90-107

Gaspers, Des et altera: Human Security ad Social Quality: Contrasts and Complementarities; The Hague: Institute of Social Studies; November 2008

Gramsci, Antonio: The Modern Prince. Essays on the Science of Politics in the Modern Age; in: Gramsci, Antonio: The Modern Prince and other writings; translated by Louis Marks; New York: International Publishers; 1957/1978: 135-188

Hart, H.L.A., 1976: Law in the Perspective of Philosophy: 1776-1976; in: New York University Law Review 51

Herrmann, Peter, 2009: Social Quality – Looking for a Global Social Policy. An Introductory Text; Taipei: NTU Social Work Review, 19/2009: 133-188

Herrmann, Peter, forthcoming: Searching for Global Policy

Herrmann, Peter: Social Professions and the State; New York: Nova, 2007

Herrmann, Peter/Dorrity, Claire: Critic of Pure Individualism; in: Dorrity/Herrmann: Social Professional Activity: The Search for a Minimum Common Denominator in Difference; New York: Nova, 2009

Holmes, Oliver Wendell, 1896: The Bar as a Profession, in: Youth's Companion, Feb. 20, 1896, reprinted in Collected Works of Justice Holmes [Sheldon M. Novick ed.], 1995; volume 3; quoted in: Sheldon M. Novick: Holmes's Path, Holmes's Goal; in: Harvard Law Review, Vol. 110, No. 5 (Mar., 1997), pp. 1028-1032

Jenkins, Iredell: Social Order and the Limits of Law. A Theoretical Essay; Princeton: Princeton University Press 1980

Kant, Immanuel, 1788: Critique of Practical Reason; Translated and Edited by Mary Gregor. With an Introduction of Andrews Reath; Cambridge: Cambridge University Press, 1997

Koslowski, Stefan, 1989: Die Geburt des Sozialstaats aus dem Geist des Deutsche Idealismus. Person und Gemeinschaft bei Lorenz von Stein; Weinheim: VCH

Luhmann, Niklas, 1993: Das Recht der Gesellschaft; Frankfurt/M.: Suhrkamp

Maris, C.W./, Jacobs, F.C.L.M., 1997: Recht, orde en Vrijheid. Een historische inleiding in de Rechtsfilosofie; Groningen: Walters-Noordhoff

Marshall, Tom H., 1959: Citizenship and Social Class; in: Citizenship and Social Class; T.H. Marshall/Tom Bottomore; London et altera: Pluto Press, 1992: 8

Marx, Karl, 1842: Proceedings of the Sixth Rhine Province Assembly. Third Article. Debates on the Law on Thefts of Wood; in: Karl Marx. Frederick Engels. Collected Works. Volume 1: Karl Marx: 1835-1843; London: Lawrence&Wishart, 1976; 224-265

Marx, Karl, 1845: Theses on Feuerbach; in: Karl Marx. Frederick Engels. Collected Works. Volume 5: Marx and Engels: 1845-1847; London: Lawrence&Wishart, 1976; 3-5

Marx, Karl, 1857-58: Economic Manuscripts of 1857-58 [First Version of the Capital]; in: in: Karl Marx. Frederick Engels. Collected Works. Volume 28: Karl Marx: 1857-1861; London: Lawrence&Wishart, 1986

Monti, Mario, 2009: Keynote address; in: European Commission. Directorate General for Economic and Financial Affairs (Ed.): Beyond the Crisis: A Changing Economic Landscape. Keynote Speeches at the Brussels Economic Forum 2009; ECFIN Economic Brief; 2. June 2009. 8-11

Otto, Hans-Uwe/Ziegler, Holger, 2008: Capabilities – Handlungsbefähigung und Verwirklichungschancen in der Erziehungswissenschaft. Der Capabilities Ansatz als neue Orientierung in der Erziehungswissenschaft. Wiesbaden: VS-Verlag

Otto, Hans-Uwe/Ziegler, Holger: 2006: Capabilities and Education; Social Work & Society; volume 4, issue 2; http://www.socwork.net/2006/2/articles/ottoziegler; 27/07/2009 7:42 p.m.

Pfaller, Alfred/Gough, Ian/Therborn, Göran [eds.], 1991: Can the Welfare state Compete? A Comparative Study of Five Advanced Capitalist Countries; Houndmills: Macmillan

Polanyi, Karl, 1944: The Great Transformation. The Political and Economic Origins of Our Time; Boston: Beacon Press, 1957

Powell, Fred, 1992: The Politics of Irish Social Policy 1600-1900; New York: Edwin Mellen Press, 1992

Preuss, Ulrich K., 1986: The Concept of Rights and the Welfare State, in: Teubner, Gunter (ed.), 1986: Dilemmas of Law in the Welfare State; Berlin/New York: Walter de Gruyter, 1986; 151-172

Schmitt, Carl, 1958: Nehmen/Teilen/Werden; in: Schmitt, Carl: Verfassungsrechtliche Aufsaetze; Berlin: Duncker&Humblot

Smith, Adam, 1759: The Theory of Moral Sentiments; Cambridge, U.K.; New York: Cambridge University Press, 2002

von Stein, Lorenz, 1869[2]: Die Verwaltungslehre. Erster Theil. Zweite Abteilung. Die Vollziehende Gewalt. Zweiter Theil: Die Selbstverwaltung und ihr Rechtssytem. Mit Vergleichung der Rechtszustände, der Gesetzgebung und Literatur in England, Frankreich und Deutschland; Stuttgart: Verlag der J.G. Cotta'schen Buchhandlung

Weinrib, Ernest Joseph, 1995: The idea of private law; Cambridge: Harvard University Press

Justice and Law Today: On the Translation of General Ideas on Justice into Claims for Security and Responsibility

Elaborated in Preparation of a Presentation on the Federal Congress of Social Work in Dortmund, Germany; September 2009

Bonitas non est pessimis esse meliorem.

Seneca

This article pleads for a change in how the question of fundamental rights is viewed. Principally these rights are at present seen as rights for protection of "inviolability". The change should be directed to creating more offensive fundamental rights that form a real greater scope of action. The point of reference for this argumentation is the social quality approach, which also makes culturally relative arguments possible.

Introduction

> *Over 200 Million children in the age between 5 and 17 years do not go to school. They go to work instead. Therefore, in June 2009, the International Trade Union Confederation (ITUC) issued a warning about a further increase in child labour.*

(ITUC,2009:2)

These days, it is generally undisputed that a certain form of injustice prevails; that things are not being done right, and as matter of fact, one would be justified to talk of screaming injustice. Yet, there is a certain unease when this issue is brought up – at least for people in my generation or in the circles I grew up; because it was instilled in us that nobody ever got harmed by hard work. Moreover, it is the best way to gather experiences for the real life. And even if we know that one cannot teach an old dog new tricks, the reality is that one learns to acquire skills for use in every day's life, rather than for the use at school. One learns best, where what is learned is practiced. Which is according to the protestant view: through work, and according to the catholic view: through grace as commanded by god.

Now in such case, the problem certainly becomes apparent. It becomes clear in the example where European insurance agents recently met to discuss which unequal treatment is justifiable. Because according to their statement the disadvantage of women within the health insurance is legitimate and the talk on fundamental rights would not be anything else than baseless talk.

But an open question, which is more or less randomly picked out comes up: What is the meaning of the fusion of a major German health insurer (*Barmer Ersatzkasse*) with other health insurances? This is just an action in their expansive process of concentration and centralization; which according to the German Ministry in charge is part of the scheme to massively limit the number of service providers in this sector. This was supposed to increase the insurers' negotiating power against doctors and hospitals. Whether is of benefit to patients is suggested to be an automatic effect but it cannot be verified whether this is the reality.

On the other hand, what do the cases of people who run amok, who obviously do not only disrespect other people's rights, but also other people's lives, got to do with human rights? This will be clearer at the end of this article – or at least it will be a little easier to think about it without generalization or lapsing into relativism.

I. Justice and Law

After this introduction that is rather playful with words, the question is more or less clear and can be divided into two parts:

1) The term justice is multi-faceted and has many connotations. Leaving the reference to the (supposedly universal) system of positive law aside, we find law as matter of the right way, righteous actions defining themselves without need of further explanation. But is it precisely in this obviousness of globality that its universality or is it its implicitness cannot be maintained. Other perceptions become directly visible; here the country road towards global unity of universal justice becomes now a highway of which the bumpiness can be fully felt. This also means that the regularities become visible: what is not obvious becomes now at least clearly visible. How can one understand something that is implicit, and from where are the relevant criteria derived from under the condition that the implications are highly ambiguous? – Child Labour – briefly mentioned above – can be clearly declared as unjust, however, this declaration is succeeded straight away by two questions: a) When is an activity defined as work as relevant in this context? b) When is such work harmful? Of course this also raises the question on how universality can be defined without destroying diversity altogether or ending in absolute relativity?

Under which conditions and in which way is "work" necessary and important for children's development?

2) How can such standards be translated into actual positive law?

In approaching these questions two steps are important. For better understanding let us take look the application of these terms in the English language. In English, there is the term *law* on one hand and the term *rights* on the other. If one looks at the usage of these terms, it becomes clear that the first term refers to a contractual figure of law while the other refers to a figuration. In his short essay *Social Process Models on Multiple Levels,* Norbert Elias describes this as a complex relationship that can be subsumed in multiple levels when he says:

> One therefore finds oneself confronted with the necessity of developing a multi-level model of society, or, if one will, a model with multiple levels, the relationships of which to one another can be presented here only as a problem, without the need to take it further in this context. It is quite clear that the process of humanity's relationship to nature, the process of human coexistence within a single survival unit such as a tribe or a state, and the process of coexistence in the form of plurality of survival units are absolutely inseparable from one another.

> *(Elias, 2009: 41)*

Of particular importance is that the common denominator of both legal dimensions is that they illustrate relations. The difference between them is that law is statutorily defined while rights are more a matter of a process. Elias however adds:

> That the human being is a process is certainly one of the most fundamental of people's experiences, but it is usually suppressed from thinking because of the overwhelming tendency of thought to reduce processes to state conditions.

> *(ibid.)*

And:

> One may say that a person passes through a process, just as one says the wind blows, although the blowing is, of course, the wind.

> *(ibid.)*

But it is worth going a step further, and emphasizing that this processuality actually means that personality itself has to be understood as process. We are not dealing with life courses but every personality is in every single moment process as s/he constitutes him/herself in every single moment by own practice.

We find an interim layer – between lawfulness and right. It is something that is commony taken for granted, remaining without explicit reflection: aside of and as part of the figure of law and the figuration of processual personalities of rights we find the form of treaties – and this includes the dimension of treatment. In other words, it is not about the determination of a relative status (as it is part of contractual agreements) nor is it a matter of acting as personality (as we see it in the case of the individual figuration). Instead we are confronted with the situation of individuals that engage together in certain processes and explicitly engage in acting together. Terms as the Latin *tractare* or the Italian *trattare* come to mind and the latter for instance translates into curing, acting, debating. Another term that frequently enters the debate on fundamental and human rights is the term *convention* – in linguistic terms a matter of agreement based on custom and/or negotiation.

Moments of status play certainly a role here, and equally relevant are moments of figurations that are based in personalities . However: They are subordinate to the stipulation of common scopes of action.

Here the following points have to be established:

First, the xyz universal human rights declaration is by no means as universal as it is commonly suggested. It is important to fully recognize this especially in the present day discussions, where this declaration has to be defended against other declarations that are based on religion. There is nothing wrong with such protection but nevertheless it is necessary to be clear that this can only occur under the perspective of a limited claim of universality.

Secondly, time and again social fundamental rights are brought forward in different debates and equally we find the question of social justice debated. However it is evident that this should be assessed with scepticism: essentially this is a heavily individualistic orientation – not founded on the tradition of 'Christian Enlightenment'.

Thirdly, the question of fundamental and human rights has strong, discursive components – and a historical character that goes beyond the question of natural law. At the same time, there is a need to ensure that this is by no means comparable to relativism.

Fourthly, this can only make sense, if we are looking for a new dimension of human rights. The common characteristics of such rights are universality and indivisibility; respect for mutual dependence and reciprocity; equality and non-discrimination; guarantee of participation and inclusion; accountability and obedience to the law. Basing fundamental rights on social quality is suggested as a fourth dimension. Social work certainly has to play a prominent role here that goes beyond defending rights. Fundamental rights should also include the right to shape social space.

II. Human Rights-Dimensions of the definition

To start with, it makes sense to take some time to look at the definition of human rights. First let us look at the universal and widely accepted definition provided by the United Nations. This partly reads as follows:

> *Human rights could be generally defined as those rights which are inherent in our nature and without which we cannot live as human beings.*

> *(United Nations, 1987: 4)*

As previously stated, general principles that reoccur time and again can be summarized by the following terms: universality and indivisibility; respect for mutual dependence and reciprocity; equality and non-discrimination; guarantee of participation and inclusion; accountability and obedience to the law.

At the same time, it is at the very least subliminally possible to take recourse to certain universal values and derived values. The cornerstone of today's legal exegesis in this area can be summarized as follows: 'Devine', i.e. law given by god, natural law and its foundation in ethical-moral terms – this is in all cases seen as *lex aeterna* of something that is independent of human beings. If we interpret activities and interests, it is about pre -and superhuman rationality, a logos and /or the human nature in itself. With this, such discussions are the least circular processes of self-justification: rights are derived from rights.

Three main points that recurringly coming to the fore:

- Equality – as a very vague and equally mystical form that has supposedly founded in natural law.
- Justice, and particularly distributional justice (e.g. Staub-Bernasconi, 2005),
- finally self-realization of the individual.

Mentioning these subjects a fundamental problem is becoming apparent. The argument is limited on a historical status quo and – paradoxically at the same time – the orientation along ideas of natural law (assumed to be ahistorical). The latter subtly and implicitly represent the compelling promise of god-given equality:

> *If we proceed on, we shall at least come out right; we shall come to the time when man came from the hand of his Maker. What was he then? Man. Man was his high and his only title and a higher cannot be given him.*

> *(Paine, 1791: 31)*

Leading to the

> *divine origins of the rights of man at the creation. Here our inquiries find a resting-place, and our reason finds a home. If a dispute about the rights of man had arisen at the distance of an hundred years from the creation, it is to this source of authority they must have referred, and it is to this same source of authority that we must now refer.*

> *(ibid.)*

Speaknig of a god-given freedom at any rate has certainly an undertone of freedom that is not really, but rather a bestowed freedom. We are facing freedom and equality that does not result from co-existence but are result of the isolation of individual creation. The idiosyncratic individualism is getting more apparent by considering the following:

> *The illuminating and divine principle of the equal rights of man (for it has its origin from the maker of man) relates, not only to the living individuals, but to generations which preceded it, by the same rule that every individual is born equal in rights with his contemporary.*

> *(ibid.: 32)*

In order to find a way out of this paradox the discussion is commonly shifted away from this problem: instead of discussing fundamental (human) rights attention is turned towards general demands for justice (see for example Reichert, 2003); minimal rights are discussed as fundamental rights or separated from defining human rights etc. At this point a big problem emerges. The question is if not every separation or differentiation leads to confusion and minimalism? And subsequently it may be asked if it would not make more sense to talk instead of fundamental social rights, based on matters of processes rather than on the principles of relations and status.

110

Another important point is the reduction of the social, more precisely, the control of the social by contractual relationship as it is getting obvious when Thomas Paine writes:

> *The fact therefore must be that the individuals themselves, each in his own personal and sovereign right, entered into a compact with each other to produce a Government: and this is the only principle on which they have a right to arise, and the only principle on which they have a right to exist.*

(Paine: 36)

Subsequently the social – and ultimately social rights too – may be seen as not much more than matters of technical and/or administrative procedures Accordingly they are defined on the basis of formal criteria rather than by their substantial criteria.

In all the three points there is at least a risk of a static orientation. The social dynamic is curiously reduced to processes of negotiation in a "dialogue on justice" (Staub-Bernasconi, 2005: 82 f.; with ref. to Shue, 1988). In other words the social itself becomes individualized and the process is restricted to negotiation of status positions and perhaps status passages.

It is also forgotten that these processes are heavily influenced by interests. A statement by Jane Addams may illustrate this:

> *Both sides can be justified in the light of the given interests: The abolition of slavery because all human beings are naturally equal or the retention of slavery because human beings are naturally and evidently unequal because of the their differences in appearances, skin colour, sex, etc. Or: For some natural law is rational law and therefore it is negotiable amongst rational people; for others it is the law emerging from instincts and therefore the rights of the strongest. Furthermore: Because reference to natural law can lead to disagreement on whether it is an uncorrupted nature of human beings, that should be put under the custody and protection of a special social organization that facilitates freedom, or whether it is a stunted, concealed, and corrupted human nature which should be tamed and disciplined. As history teaches, the second perception delivers time and again the legitimation for the establishment or consolidation of a regime of government and chastisement against the majority in order to protect the freedom of a minority. And lastly the idea of natural law often leads to the perception of inherent rights for those who already*

enjoy them instead of the idea of fighting for the rights for those who don't have them.

(Addams, 1912; cited from: Staub-Bernasconi, without date)

Things get actually complicated in theory as well as in practice when we try to understand social passages as passages of individuals in the social sphere and also as a historical passage of the social, because these can actually only be understood as interests in concrete developmental contexts. At this point Silvia Staub-Bernasconi's surely reasonable assessment falls short and leads to a minimalistic concept – they propose the following :

Human- and Social rights are real Utopias

> *a) because it can be clearly indicated to which common human needs they can be linked and at the same time in which widely strewn knowledge of human- and social science they must be developed and integrated into an interdisciplinary theory of needs...;*

> *b) because sensibility to human misery, e.g. the crying of children, the scream of those who are humiliated, imprisoned, tortured, raped, the apathies of those who are starving, jobless (deMause1977; Honig1992; Müller1992) does suffice to develop an understanding, and does not need any recourse to seemingly eternally applicable, superhuman values, norms and theories in terms of higher humanity;*

> *c) because one can state the physical, psychological socio-economic and cultural conditions and the political decisions on whose basis the needs could be fulfilled;*

> *d) because they are binding, anchored central components of international law since 1992 and lastly,*

> *e) because one can inform oneself – at least where citizens rights to freedom and defence are concerned – which conventions, articles, paragraphs and supplementary protocol they can invoke in the case of infringement, which legal proceedings to initiate and which panels and commissions are in charge of compliance and monitoring, i.e one is aware of a concrete course of action.*

(ibid: 9)

As undoubtedly as these points are, it is proposed to look for an approach that argues more positively – and if you like – an approach that does not

112

wait until for crying and screams to proclaim their right not to cry but rather one that proclaims the right to laugh and be happy from the outset.

III. Approaching Social Law

It is evident, that we find ourselves in an area that is full of tensions and that has been time and again revisited by social scientists: it was already seen as a problem of personal relationships by Aristotle, as moment of legal development by Henry James Sumner Maine; as a question of economic systems by Ferdinand Tönnies and in Max Weber's or Jürgen Habermas' opinions it had been looked at as an overarching principle of societal relationships.

In a comparative perspective, looking from the angle of socio-political practice at these matters one point becomes clear – although we are at least in Europe-centrist perspective dealing with a secular process: In German tradition we have a definition of rights that is heavily contractual, the English tradition has a theoretical figurative orientation on rights, while in the French tradition one would rather speak of a genuine social law in terms of a 'people's contract'. Thereby one has to discharge certain terms that suggest the contrary: the French term *contrat social,* the English treaties and treatises and the German insurance principles ('Versicherungsprinzipien') create a different understanding than what they are presenting in reality.[52]

A common factor is that in all three systems a process of jurisdiction provides the foundation. On the other hand, this example also illustrates hugely different principles of implementation.

It is fo crucial importance to realize that after all we are dealing with a bureaucratic system that determines the rules – based on specific instrumental reasoning:

> *Knowledge and rationality were curtailed in a very specific way: by prioritising the evaluation of costs and neglecting impact studies ; by prioritising benefit systems and disregarding the burden of fees and taxes; by the irreconcilable distance between economic and non-economic views; but above all, by the real negation of balanced reasoning, i.e the balancing of the pros and cons of the welfare-state.*

(Zacher, 2008: 135)

---

[52] Such classification and allocation plays only a heurisitc roll, reference to specific historical ideals and ideals of the course of development.

Even more important is Zacher's reference to the particularity of the welfare state. He explicitly refers to the particularity of the process of political negotiation. To him, it is about 'social sharing' – or also the 'not taking-away'; the preference of the 'middle voters´ and the subordination under the cycle of elections' (see ibid.: 138 f).

This implies a much deeper particularity, which Zacher also addresses, but does not subsume under this heading; it is the evolution of today's system, which is commonly taken for given without need of further consideration. For one, these are normative backgrounds that are assumed as given:

> *For us the welfare state is something that is taken as matter of course:*
>
> * *through its historical development*
>
> * *from norms that lay ahead of its coming into force,*
>
> * *and lastly from the constitutional concept of a social and democratic federal state, based on the rule of law.*
>
> *(ibid.: 130)*

On the other hand, the specific rationality is characterized by certain negativity.

> *It was about exceptions. The groups for which the welfare state existed were those who had been disadvantaged. The benefits that it provided had been oriented along the subnormal.*
>
> *(ibid.: 132)*

A third particularity can also be discerned from Zacher's statements: It is the orientation of the welfare state, to the prevailing circumstances, to continuity and safeguarding this continuity. In essence, it is about something that has already been anchored in the core of contractual creation. In the case where the contract is an agreement between two parties, bound to deliver or produce (a product or a service), mutual obligations and mutual benefit are its central features. A further central feature is that these obligations and benefits are limited to what is explicitly specified in the agreement.

Therefore it is only logical that the following applies when we look at the welfare state:

The most important consequences of this system...are the following three:

- *First: the precedence of particular, mostly group-related interests over a general consideration ...*

- *Secondly: the precedence of 'agreed' evaluation of social needs over the empirical investigation*

- *Thirdly: the precedence of the existing order over the future order, the vested rights over the necessities, the interested parties of today over the interested parties of the day after tomorrow.*

(ibid.: 139 f.)

However the following perspectives are thereby important – Hans F. Zacher describes these in his deliberations over the basic types of social rights that can be found in the two origins of 'social' thinking in Europe:

- The issue of poverty – carried on from the middle ages into the modern era – developed along the line of exclusion/ inclusion

- For the social question if is characteristic that labourers:

lived on the border of inclusion and exclusion. Although they had property, the property was largely guarded and inaccessible. The 'social question' was a question on the position of a specific group in the society, a 'class question'.

(Zacher, 1993: 258)

This becomes especially interesting, when apart from the secular aspect one also looks at the differences in the actual 'handling' of relevant issues. This cannot be undertaken exhaustively – but a quick glance into three examples appears informative – they can be found in the following array:

COUNTRY	SOCIO-ECONOMIC TRADITION	SOCIO-PHILOSOPHICAL TRADITION	UNDERTANDING OF SOCIAL LAW
Germany	Corporatist capitalism	Amalgamation of the principles instrumental and absolute rationality	Social corporatist constitutional state with welfare -tendencies--- „law but few rights"
England	Strict free market fundamentalism"	Utilitarism	Common law und charity based 'educational state' --- 'rights as given by nature'
France	Indicative planning of a central system where state owned corporation play a big role	Humanism	'solidarity oriented state based on the rule of law' --- 'rights as citizens rights'

Overview 1

If one looks at the finality, as had been briefly mentioned earlier – when looking at divine law or with a view on reasoning oriented along the argument of natural law – and when one considers how finality is now propagated within the national frameworks with of the claim of absolute validity one can see that the development of the system itself will ultimately move towards a quasi-autopoietic circularity that sooner or later brings itself to the limits of the intrinsic rules. From being originally a welfare state for the marginalized it tends to develop towards a social system that can be categorized in terms of social quality.

Social quality is characterised by the degree to which people are able to participate in social relationships and being so under conditions that elevate the quality of their lives, widens their individual horizons and does so in a dialectical relationship. This self-enhancement results in a mutual widening of interaction. The determining factors are socio-economic security, inclusion, cohesion and empowerment. Thus social policy becomes indeed understandable as politics of socialization.

All in all, it is not only the sphere of influence that has broadened due to diverse reasons, but also the objective reasoning - a tendency that has already in the past been caused by some underlying measures: the creation of a social system, where the state is not a helping entity but rather an instance of socialization. This can be better expressed by referring to Norbert Elias. Interdependence is already laid out in the multi-layered system. This is not only a matter of contractual dependence but also a matter of constitutional dependence. However, again we have to note the following contradiction:

> *The sense of dependence in certain personal relationships has been lessened by social welfare and other social benefits; the risks of life are becoming increasingly socialized and secured by statutory provisions, guaranteed across all societal groups, so that for instance the dependence of women from men is minimized. Subsequently the state has taken over the role previously held primary societal institutions such as the family, minimising the dependence on them (cf. Elias 1988[3]: 274). Individuals receiving state benefits enhances their ability to act and increases their mobility; the detachment of individuals' life course from collective and traditional contexts is increased. The establishment of a welfare state promotes and facilitates individualization 'on the foundation of stable incomes and steady*

services of general interest[53]'. (Mayer/Mueller 1989: 47)

(Ebers, 1995: 245; with reference to: Elias, 1988[3]; Mayer/Mueller, 1989)

The full enforcement of these principles was actually only possible thanks to the reasoning of the Enlightenment period. The legal terms in that period were purely individualistic and in the interest of the bourgeoisie in goods, money and profit . They were only sugar-coated by the reference to the trinity of freedom, equality and brotherhood.

Turned positively this means – this will be crucial for the later deliberations - that a change is required in the reasoning of social- and welfare states. If one traces the societal development in broad terms, it can be charazterised as move from direct barter, to tributary societies (as depicted by Samir Amin [s. Amin, 1988]), moving further to capitalist economies. Exchange and contribution are in this case both economic as well welfare-related principles. However this means that a fourth level – according to a 'new division justice' should be looked for. In developing this argument further a concept is proposed under the heading of social quality based in social justice. It (i) builds on a different understanding of social rights and (ii) explicitly includes human rights. This means as well to turn away from a thinking that today's social- and welfare state should refer to the poverty- and social question or is solely referring to these traditional roots.

---

[53] The original speaks of 'stetiger Daseinsfürsorge "

118

Societal Characterization	Accumulation Regime	Regulation of Welfare
Direct barter (hunter and- gatherer-economies)	Economies depending on direct metabolism with nature and oriented on satisfying immediate needs	Mutual support
Tributary societies	Surplus production to satisfy needs of lords	Parochial clientelism
Capitalist market societies	Mass production and mass consumption as foundation of concentration and centralization of capital, constituting far-reaching networks of dependency. At the same time niche economy	Social- and welfare state founded in employment
Finance and service market capitalism	Individualized und diversified mass consumption as foundation for extreme concentration und centralization of capital with far-reaching and global networks of dependency. At the same time niche economy	Marginalized social- und welfare state, founded in employment but with growing privatization and precarity
National social economies	Social economy: flexible mass production in small localized production units	Social quality based in social justice

Overview 2

IV. Human rights – Social rights – Social work

This finds a particularly clear expression by the fact when time and again the focus is on support mechanisms of individuals. This is also the case when we orient on functionings as Amarty Sen does, in the case of capability approach. This is a fundamentally individualistic perspective the core of which aims on broadening the real freedoms of the individual (s. Bonvin, 2009: 10).

> *The determining factor is that the capability perspective requires a combination of both dimensions of freedom: The broadening of a great deal of valued opportunities is complemented by the capability to express individual preferences, wishes and expectations and to lend them substance.*
>
> *(ibid.: 12)*

However, this statement also reveals that the need for collective practice and structural changes of society is ignored. Though integration into the labour market is not presented as sole perspective, Sen's understanding of economic processes is mainly influenced by classical understanding and focuses on the surveillance of:

> *market transactions, unconstrained concealment of information, or unregulated use of activities that allow the powerful to capitalize on an asymmetrical advantage*
>
> *(Sen, 1999: 142).*

After all, it is solely a question of market integration. What appears in the perspective of social work laudable, emerges in a wider socio-political and political-economic perspective as danger of liberal individualistic measures,. Ultimately it is about development of individual freedom and not about development of societal justice, responsibility and security. To be extreme, one could simply say that, "there is no such thing as society".[54/55]

Indeed most of these debates are in one form or another based on rights. For instance much work within the scope of the so-called developmental cooperation or the European Social Charter. Similarly, the reference to

---

[54] Evidently an allusion to Margaret Thatcher's statement in Women's Own magazine, October 31 1987 – http://briandeer.com/social/thatcher-society.htm; 27.09.09 9:21:54 a.m.

[55] See further critic in Herrmann, 2009; Gaspers et altera, 2008

universal principles is increasingly issued in academic debates – for example in Amartya Sen's work as well in the work of those who adopt his reflections on the so called developed societies (Otto/Ziegler, 2008; 2006). Of course such debates do not only take place in the western world but also in Asia and Latin America albeit in other forms. At the same time, these references remain very general and 'basic'. Concrete-general reflections on the universal principles of human rights as they had been described above are replaced by arguments on plausibility.

On the other hand there are clear indications that insights in operational perspectives narrowed dramatically: Recent discussions clearly reveal that, such legal issues no longer really pose a question: For example in the area of antidiscrimination the main concerns are in the current debate in Germany the benefits and costs of the Equal Treatment Act (Allgemeines Gleichbehandlungsgesetz) (s. Priddat/Wilms, 2008). As mentioned in the beginning, there is some unequal treatment in the insurance sector that is accepted to be justifiable and that is supposed to be natural. In a workshop of EU-NGOs representatives from the European Women's Lobby reported recently that under the impression of the crisis women's rights and the principles of equal treatment were typically seen as matters of discretion. This shows how important the juridification of even fundamental rights is, in the sense of positive regulation, and at the same time it shows that reasoning in the perspectives of ethics and natural law is bound to fail, because ethics are limited to capitalistic ethics, which neither the Catholic nor the Protestant church want to question nor would be able to question. Certainly, a European human rights commissioner, an idea brought into discussion by José Manuel Barroso in 2009, may quite possibly offer a ray of hope. But such a position may also mean that human- and fundamental rights issues remain external: something artificial that has nothing to do with other political areas and most importantly has then nothing to do with the economic system as an original social relationship. And carried to the extreme human rights issues could be assigned to foreign policy rather than internal affairs.

With the above said, a demand that appears new, which is at the very least neglected in explicit discussions on social- and human rights is being made to social work. :Let us have a look into one of the standard works in this area: Elisabeth Reichert's *Social Work and Human Rights. A Foundation for Policy and Practice (Reichert, 2003)*. It is evident that the essential issue is always the safeguarding of human rights as it reads:

Like social justice, definitions of human rights can also present open-ended responses. However, human rights encompass a more comprehensive and defined set of guidelines for social work practice than social justice. Human rights focus on what must be given to a client, which elevates the discussion into one not simply of recognizing the needs of a client but also of effectively satisfying those needs.

(ibid.: 13)

Jim Ife appeals for a discursive approach and starts from the supposition that

Rights are constructed through human interaction and an ongoing dialogue about what should constitute a common humanity.

(Ife, 2001: 6)

And together with Lucy Fiske he elaborates that:

Legislation does not determine people's belief systems; this can be better achieved through a process of conscientisation and ongoing dialogue. It is here, in developing and facilitating the human rights discourse, that there are important contributions to be made by other disciplinary understandings. Human rights become more 'human' and more robust in a multidisciplinary discourse.

(Ife/Fiske, 2003: 1)

Additionally in an article with the title *How to Rethink Theories of Social Work in the Light of Human Rights*, Silvia Staub-Bernasconi urges for a third mandate for social work. Apart from assistance and monitoring she introduces a third factor which can be best described as ethical self-determination.

A profession (Profession) has a triple mandate which consists of both already mentioned mandates from clients and society as well as a third one. And this has the following components:

- *a scientific description and explanation base for its methods, which are reliable to solve or prevent social problems, and*

- *an ethical base, i.e. a professional code of ethics which is – in the case of social work – explicitly oriented on human rights and social justice.*

Both elements lead to an autonomously defined mandate by the profession itself and – if necessary – to the modification or refusal of mandates from the agency as well as from clients in ethical or/and scientific terms. (Staub-Bernasconi, 2009: 4)

Once and for all, by now it should be clear that the character of such rights must be described as being centrally about processes. This means that the regulation of such rights must also result from a social process.

This means on the other hand that social work as human rights science – apart from being a protective authority – must establish itself as authority that defines these social provisions.

Elisabeth Reichert urges us three guidelines should be followed when concretely accessing human rights questions, namely;

- *Examine the history of the cultural practice. ...*

- *Examine the powerbrokers who determined the cultural norm. ...*

- *Examine the cultural norm within a contemporary human rights standard.*

(Reichert, 2007: 10)

Thus first and foremost it should be established in which manner the term 'rights' should be engaged – both in academic discussions and practical social work. If one follows some of the discussants, the goal is at present to democratically develop the discourse on social and fundamental rights again. This proceeds from the allegation that this discourse is presently occupied by neo-liberal school of thought. In actual fact a clear understanding of 'rights-based politics' should be elaborated in the first place. During the Renaissance and later the Age of Enlightenment, the discourse was fully directed towards individualism. Accordingly even the understanding of the social had been suggested to be a matter of supporting individualism and individual personal fulfilment. This is also the concept that underlies social policy in industrial societies: an individualist and individualizing concept of social rights. However it is essential to develop an understanding of social rights that is radically social. A first step has already been suggested in a different area and proposes the following benchmarks:

- *appropriateness as*
  - ➤ *'availing of property'[56] and*
  - ➤ *adequacy and*
- *equality as*

---

[56] This should not be confused with property generation under private law.

> *contestable legitimacy ('control of the system') and*

> *empowerment in terms of developing capabilities ('control of the own life and development')*

(Herrmann/Dorrity, 2009: 14)

This results in the following areas of conflict and/or horizons of possibilities:

		appropriation	
		property	adequacy
equality	legitimacy		
	empowerment		

(ibid.)

Overview 3

This means that it is relatively easy to arrive at a determination. A central dimension, emerging from the social quality approach has to be seen in the orientation on empowerment. The question of power, which is implicitly addressed, has two dimensions, namely: (i) the actual doing and (ii) the potential to do i.e the dimension of the possible. Obviously, the example of Obama clearly shows that it is not enough to declare 'Yes we can', as we are dealing at least also with the question of power differentials.

In the perspective of the legal system it is essential that positive law always requires a concretely given and unalterable social connection.

Positive law assumes an ordered social context that exhibits certain deficiencies: it envisages more desirable – an ideal – ordering of the context; it prescribes the steps to be taken in order to move the actual towards the ideal; and it orders that these measures be instituted. That is, positive law is at once expository, normative prescriptive, advisory, and imperative. But it is positive law as a means to an end ...

(Jenkins, 1980: 75)

The question is how the two different legal dimensions – rights and law – can be merged. A reference to Ernst Bloch offers such an opportunity. In his book *The principle of Hope,* he illustrates the following layers of what is possible: The formally possible, the factually-objectively possible, the objectively possible as emerging from the object and the achievable (s. Bloch, 1959: 258-288; cf. Herrmann, forthcoming).

V. The demand for real social law.

At first glance the situation appears to be clear.: there is a clear differentiation or separation: The basic figure of righteousness as 'right' is the convention while the basic figure 'law' is a contract. But strictly read the convention is open to unlimited relativism and exercising arbitrary power while only the 'law' is binding – we can see this already in the Leges Duodecim Tabularum (Zwölftafelgesetz; see. http://www. hsaugsburg.de/~harsch/Chronologia/Lsante05/LegesXII/leg_ta00.html – 27.09.09 11:18:18 a.m.), later in the German twelve volumes of the Social Code or later again in the German Social Code in its present form (see http://bundesrecht.juris.de/bundesrecht/GESAMT_a.html#S; see under SGB - 27.09.09 11:23:27 a.m.; http://www.sozialgesetzbuch-sgb.de/ – 27.09.09 11:22:01 a.m.) [57]

Demands for rights-based approaches in social politics certainly have a fatally paradoxical effect. Strictly taken it presents a demand for a despotic rule. And indeed we find this frequently in human rights debates. Looking at the ruling in the case Leyla Şahin v. Turkey (European Court of Human Rights 2004 and 2005), it becomes clear how many different dimensions and levels had been considered. And above all, every single argument in this case was intended to protect different interests and safe guard respective power positions.

however if looked at from a socio-political perspective, this can hardly be accepted because here human rights issues simply emerge as power issues (in actually fact they are power issues) and become issues of subjective assessment, depending on a specific cultural context. What remains to be done?

---

[57] In connection to this it is important to note that although the law is uncontestable and does not need interpretation, as long as it is precise, it is at the same time important to recognise that precision is by no means equal to wholeness.

The development of human rights is generally regarded as a result of three steps, namely (i) defence and non-interference rights (freedom, equality, brotherhood and negative rights for the benefit of the aspiring bourgeoisie); (ii) rights of entitlement as positive rights of individuals; (iii) collective and minority rights.

Here it is suggested to add a fourth layer that helps on one hand overcoming the subjectivism of commonly accepted relative positions and overcoming on the other hand the character of conventional human rights definitions; the aim is to facilitate and necessitate a translation to positive law. The latter would also mean actual socialisation of social law.

Law is generally part of a wider societal process, which is normative in the form of defining norms but also following and executing norm. The reference to norms is often construed subjectively as an issue of ethically-based procedures. In such formulation one could see it as positive formulation of morally based approaches as they are usually brought forward in old nursery books.

These norms are above all a reflection or an expression of the complex mutual relationship of human beings and of their to their material and organic environment. It is still legitimate to speak of law as reflection of relations of production. In a wider historical perspective, this can be classified into the following stages:

Approach to Reality	Approach to Law
Immediate appropriation of nature	Spontaneous natural law – as law of nature ('environmental law')
Successive division of labour	Divine law
Successive division of control	Canon law[58]
Emergence of systems of communal production[59]	Common law
Heavily exchange based economies and societies emphasising the importance of 'civic-ness' as distinct area	Beginning with the Lex Duodecim Tabularum the Roman law and the later civil law
Prospected social quality society	Global Human Rights Approach

(Berman/Herrmann, Systems of Law and Social Quality; in: Social & Public Policy Review; Social & Public Policy Review, 2012; 6, 1, pp. 20-39 -
http://www.uppress.co.uk/socialpolicy_pdf/Berman%20herman.pdf)

Overview 4

VI. Conclusions and outlook.

The distinction can be seen in line with a distinction made at an earlier stage, namely presented in overview Overview 2. We are looking at the classification of rights not as absolute rights but as relative rights. However, relative is not meant to deal with abstract assessments and definitions, but in the understanding of real, i.e. objective conditions and spaces of opportunities and thus socio-economic practice. These are not given as matters of individual self-realisation or by way of subjective values. And they are not given on grounds of externally defined norms or as matter of 'eternally valid ethics'. Decisive is a systematically developed understanding of the social. This was mentioned above briefly in connection with the view on social quality as well as the outlining of horizons of the possible as presented by Ernst Bloch.

This is therefore once again an appeal for an approach that consciously departs from the minimalistic view of human rights and focuses instead on a wider formulation of social rights. This implies a strict rejection of all forms of relativism, since it is not about cultural provisions or provisions on abstract norms. Neither is the individual seen as focal point

---

[58] Though in a wider understanding, as law of religious bodies/institutions
[59] Though well going hand in hand with a separation of power and control, thus including feudal and especially capitalist systems

nor is an abstract concept of the social taken as point of reference – as for instance as state or as an imaginary public interest. On the contrary, it is about capturing spontaneity of relations and processes in their continuous practice. This is something that is challenging if seen in the light of a social science that suggests even the social as determined by individualism.

Although a certain form of relativism does indeed play a role, the said includes an orientation that may perhaps be seen as the opposite (though not necessarily as a claim of absoluteness or even absolutism). The goal of the presented deliberations is to take a step away from a purely defensive understanding of human and fundamental rights. They should be understood as rights that create integrity and not rights that protect integrity.

Going back to the beginning: Why do the cases of the person who runs amok and the merger of health insurers play a role? They can serve as examples of two complementary extremes radically characterising the trend of individualism. One case is about creation of market conditions: The individual is left defenceless by these market conditions as rights are converted to contract law. Seen in this light, it is of course about widening rights, only that care should be taken that this complex system of contractual relationships is limited. We can say that this is the establishment of institutionalized individualism. The second case is one of sheer individualism. Such cases are normally discussed from two perspectives. Some view this as plain injustice by the individual while others may attempt to 'comprehend', 'explain' this misconduct. However such comprehension of individual capacities is limited because individual wellbeing as well as quality of life is easier to understand as a complex failure of the system. Such individualistic reflexivity will always make it easy to attribute their failures to the other.

References

Addams, Jane, 1912; zitiert nach: Staub-Bernasconi, without date

Amin, Samir, 1988: Eurocentrism; New York: Monthly Review Press, 1989; Originally as L'Eurocentrime. Critique d'une Ideologie; Paris: Anthropos, 1988

Berman, Yitzhak/Herrmann, Peter, 2012: Systems of Law and Social Quality; in: Social & Public Policy Review; Social & Public Policy Review, 2012; 6, 1, pp. 20-39 http://www.uppress.co.uk/socialpolicy_pdf/Berman%20herman.pdf

Bloch, Ernst, 1959: Prinzip Hoffnung; Frankfurt/M: Suhrkamp [geschrieben 1938-1947; überarbeitet 1953 and 1959]

Bonvin, Jean-Michel, 2009: Der Capability Ansatz und sein Beitrag für die Analyse gegenwärtiger Sozialpolitik; in: SP. Soziale Passagen. Journal für Empirie und Theorie Sozialer Arbeit; Wiesbaden: Verlag für Sozialwissenschaften: Heft 1: 8-22

Ebers, Nicola, 1995: Individualisierung. Georg Simmel – Norbert Elias – Ulrich Beck; Würzburg: Königshausen&Neumann

Elias, Norbert, 1980/81: Social Process Models on Multiple Levels; in: Elias, Norbert: Essays III. On Sociology and the Humanities; Dublin: University College Dublin Press, 2009: 40-42

Elias, Norbert, 1988[3]: Die Gesellschaft der Individuen; hrsg. V. Michael Schroeter, Frankfurt/M.

Europäischer Gerichtshof für Menschenrechte, 2005: Şahin gegen die Türkei, Antrag Nr. 44774/98, Urteil der Kammer vom 29. Juni 2004

Gaspers, Des et altera, 2008: Human security and social quality: contrasts and complementaries/by Des Gasper, Laurent J.G. van der Maesen, Thanh-Dam Truong, Alan Walker; Den Haag: ISS-Working Paper, 462

Große Kammer, 2005: Urteil vom 10. November 2005; s. http://www.humanrights.ch/home/upload/pdf/051110_EGMR_sahinvsturkey.pdf - 27.09.09 11:32:51 a.m.

Herrmann, Peter, 2009: Social Quality – Looking for a Global Policy Approach. A Contribution to the Analysis of the Development of Welfare States; Bremen: Europaeischer Hochschulverlag

Herrmann, Peter, forthcoming: Searching for Global Social Policy – Economy, Economics and Governance

Herrmann, Peter/Dorrity, Claire, 2009: Critic of Pure Individualism; in: Dorrity/ Herrmann: Social Professional Activity: The Search for a Minimum Common Denominator in Difference; New York: Nova

Ife, Jim, 2001: Human Rights and Social Work; Cambridge: Cambridge University Press

Ife, Jim/Fiske, Lucy, 2003: Institutional and Residual Conceptions of Human Rights; Activating Human Rights and Diversity Conference Byron Bay, NSW, July – http://info.humanrights.curtin.edu.au/local/docs/IRConceptions.pdf; 18/09/2009 8:49 p.m.

IGB, 2009: IGB warnt. Kurzmeldung; in: soli aktuell. Newsletter der DGB-Jugend; Hrsg.: DGB Jugend: Ausgabe Juli 2009: Berlin: DGB-Bundesvorstand, 2009

Jenkins, Iredell, 1980: Social Order and the Limits of Law. A Theoretical Essay; Princeton: Princeton University Press

Mayer, Karl Ulrich/Mueller, Walter, 1989: Lebensverläufe im Wohlfahrtsstaat; in Weymann, Ansgar [Hrsg.]: Handlungsspielräume. Untersuchungen zur Individualisierung und Institutionalisierung von Lebensläufen in der Moderne; Stuttgart: 41-60

Otto, Hans-Uwe/Ziegler, Holger, 2008: Capabilities – Handlungsbefähigung und Verwirklichungschancen in der Erziehungswissenschaft. Der Capabilities Ansatz als neue Orientierung in der Erziehungswissenschaft. Wiesbaden: VS-Verlag

Otto, Hans-Uwe/Ziegler, Holger: 2006: Capabilities and Education; Social Work & Society; volume 4, issue 2; http://www.socwork.net/2006/2/articles/ottoziegler; 27/07/2009 7:42 p.m.

Paine, Thomas, 1791: Rights of Man; With an Introduction by Derek Matravers; Hertfordshire: Wordsworth, 1976

Priddat, Birger/Wilms, Heinrich, 2008: Nutzen und Kosten des Allgemeinen Gleichbehandlungsgesetzes (AGG). Teil I Analyse und Bewertung der Studie „Gesetzesfolgekosten des Allgemeinen Gleichbehandlungsgesetzes'; Berlin: Antidiskrimierungsstelle des Bundes; www.antidiskriminierungsstelle.de

Reichert, Elisabeth, 2003: Social Work and Human Rights. A Foundation for Policy and Practice; New York: Columbia University Press

Reichert, Elisabeth, 2007: Challenges in Human Rights: A Social Work Perspective; New York: Columbia University Press

Sen, Armatya, 1999: Development as Freedom. Oxford: Oxford University Press:

Shue, Henry, 1988: Basic Rights. Subsistence, Affluence, and US Foreign Policy; Princeton/New Jersey: Princeton University Press

Staub-Bernasconi, Silvia, 2005: Gerechtigkeit und Sozialer Wandel; in: Thole, Werner: Soziale Arbeit im Öffentlichen Raum; Wiesbaden: VS Verlag für Sozialwissenschaften: 75-87

Staub-Bernasconi, Silvia, 2009: How to Rethink Theories of Social Work in the Light of Human Right. Pre-Conference 'Human Rights in Teaching and Practice', April 26th; ENSACT-Conference in Dubrovnik/Croatia: Social Action in Europe. Different Legacies – Common Challenges. April 27th to April 29th, 2009 - http://www.ensact.eu/conferences/Dubrovnik/Presentations/8Luna/Session5W18/HUMAN_RIGHTS_AND_THEIR_RELEVANCE_FOR_SW.pdf; 18/09/2009 7:50 p.m.:

130

Staub-Bernasconi, without date: Das fachliche Selbstverständnis Sozialer Arbeit –
Wege aus der Bescheidenheit Soziale Arbeit als Human Rights Profession 7 -
http://www.sw.fh-koeln.de/akjm/iks/dl/ssb.pdf - 19.09.09 4:44 p.m.

United Nations, 1987: Human rights: questions and answers; New York: United
Nations

Zacher, Hans F., 1993: Grundtypen des Sozialrechts; in: Zacher, Hans F.:
Abhandlungen zum Sozialrecht; Baron von Maydell, Bernd/Eichenhofer,
Eberhard [Hrsg.]; Heidelberg: C.F. Mueller Juristischer Verlag: 257-278

Zacher, Hans F., 2008: Die Dilemmata des Wohlfahrtsstaates; in: Zacher, Hans F.:
Abhandlungen zum Sozialrecht II; Becker, Ulrich/Ruland, Franz [Hrsg.];
Heidelberg: C.F Mueller Verlag: 129-141

Human Rights: For Sale or Saviour in the Globalising Market Economy

Text Elaborated in the Preparation of a Presentation on Occasion of the Hundred-Years Anniversary Celebration of The National Social Policy Association in Finland; Kuopio; October 2009[60]

Ignoranti, que portum petat, nullus suusventus est

Seneca

Abstract

Thank you for the invitation – I am very pleased to be here. So to say as young Fin: trying to learn by putting forward some ideas that allow me to learn from your reactions and deliberations. And I am definitely not here as German – the country where I spent a large part of my life, the country as well of the post-WWII-Wirtschaftswunder, the economic miracle after WWII; nor do want I talk here as Irish – representing a county where I spent in the meantime another large trunk of my life, and the country which had been known for some time as representative of a boosting economy: the Celtic tiger, and now gaining fame on the grounds of having failed to keep even a tiny cat alive.

Both successes – and both later relative failures – can be traced back to fundamentally a very similar pattern of which the fundamental feature, so the argument of the present contribution: the fundamental individualism of market based economies, in which the social remains subordinated, takes the form of an add-on and then becomes artificial. This undermines as well the character of a more fundamental approach towards Human Rights and the recognition of the need for shifting the debate towards a different understanding of the economic process.

---

[60] My special Thanks go to Juhani Laurinkari who made it possible for me to put the debate into an excitingly new context. Thank You as well to Juho Saari for his remarks as 'commentator' during the congress, some of which are reflected in the present version.

132

Introduction: Why look at one problem if we can have three?

The biggest problem is not to let people accept new ideas, but to let them forget the old ones.

(John Maynard Keynes)

It may come along as strange coincidence: in 1989, Francis Fukuyama heralded the end of history and not even 20 years later we face a revival of history, capitalism in its supposedly "cleanest form": a capitalism which had been arguably a purely "technical mechanisms, liberated from any ideological ballast" presents itself as expanse of rubble – all the trouble due to a bubble. If we actually look at the current situation, there is a paradox: Though we apparently regain history, we do so only falling back on historical patterns, patterns that are well known from history. However, the understanding of history does not follow the understanding of history as development made and controlled by man. As such, the reappearance of history on the agenda is somewhat contradicting those principles from which it arose. But still, it is as well the development of historical consciousness in terms of an emerging need that we have to control history; that we are responsible for the development and furthermore for showing that alternatives actually do exist – leaving for a while the two questions open (though they can never be really left open): Who are we? And: What kind of alternatives do we look for?

Of course, we may ask to which extent people ever made their own history – when the revolution successfully ended and life normalised, the new phase had been characterised by reinterpreting the liberty of rights into the freedom of contracts, the redefinition of equality on the basis of exchange and the understanding of fraternity in its capitalised form: as matter of social capital.

It may seem rather provocative to some. And to others it may appear being too abstract: we all have to cope with our daily struggles and these are characterised by such requirements of contracts, exchange and the need to engage with other: invest (in) social capital in order to overcome the demands of immediate issues. It is then actually in two ways that the burst of the bubble left a field of rubble: an economic crisis that goes far beyond the standards known by our contemporaries; and a debris of different ideas, suggestions of overcoming the current situation, some more pointing on technical fallacies, others suggesting the need for a more principal change. Taking a human rights perspective in this context points on two areas that are of special importance:

- Politically, the raising fundamentalism – including in terms of policy development and also in terms of economic strategies different kind of retrenchment approaches;

- Economically, the partial resurgence of orientations towards a more controlled, steered economy on the one hand and on the other hand the emphasis of decentralised and responsible economies.

And it is not by chance that we find following merits praised this year by the receiving the Nobel-Prize: in economics (i) the "analysis of economic governance, especially the commons" (Elinor Ostrom); (ii) the "analysis of economic governance, especially the boundaries of the firm" (Oliver E. Williamson); for peace: (iii) the "extraordinary efforts to strengthen international diplomacy and cooperation between peoples" (Barack Obama) – which is probably more meant to be the application of diplomacy rather than crude violence in defence of the American dream; and for literature (IV) for the effort by Herta Müller "who, with the concentration of poetry and the frankness of prose, depicts the landscape of the dispossessed".

We know poverty again and we know that overcoming poverty needs more than trust in a liberal market society. Still, to me one thing is striking: With all the moaning and with all the efforts to overcome the raising problems there is a lack of readiness to really look into the economic problems of the current crisis. And furthermore, there is a rather fundamental lack of look into the question of how to develop a rights-based approach. We can go even a step further: in different veins we find a re-subjectivation of matters of the causes, effects and necessary consequences: charity instead of rights, complain about a lack of responsibility rather than seeing the current situation as consequent perseverance of the principles of the chosen economic model; and search for a global moral consensus without, however, accepting the right of benefit in equal terms. In this context we find as well – sometimes frantic – attempts and searches for solutions of very different kind. Though politically highly problematic to mention them together, we find religious fundamentalism, religious or value-conservative reflections or alternative economic approaches, searching for ways of change, emerging from small-scale niche productions. It is surely interesting to discuss in detail the different instances. However, it seems to be equally valuable to look at the different perspectives more from a birds perspective, trying (i) to make out fundamental flaws of the current debate and (ii) defining some core pillars for a way forward. For me, addressing this congress, part of the 100 years celebration of the Social Policy Association of Finland, means to take up an age-old debate, trying to overcome the split which we see today throughout different arrays: the triangularisation of Western, capitalist societies and thinking – a triangularisation that comes along in different forms: the market, the state and the family or the communities; science, social science and somewhat in the middle: economics as a kind of "exact social science"; the distinction between state, contract and regulating instance – usually seen as developmental pattern but also to be seen as pattern of different simultaneously existing patterns of integration (cf. Herrmann, 2009); the trias politica of the separation of powers; the division of rights, according to Tom H. Marshall a matter of the historical development from civil, to political and social rights and not least to first footprints of western modernity: liberté, égalité, fraternité – perhaps all going back to the holy trinity as it is characteristic for Christianity. But it may be as well the consequence of a rather mechanical understanding of dialectics as simplified version of thesis, antitheses and synthesis.

Looking for a perspective – not least a perspective in developing more appropriate policy answers – means first and foremost to analyse where all these separations actually have their origin.

Let me start by looking at a division that I consider as being most fundamental – having even a kind of anthropological dimension to it: the division between and even separation of science, social science and practice. Using the terms science I do actually not mean anything like it in our current understanding. Rather, I mean first the fact that human beings developed the ability to abstract planning processes – thinking – from immediate practice, later going further by splitting the way of thinking itself, looking for the technical solution for upcoming tasks (here and now and as well as matter of developing an understanding of time) – the objective or instrumental reason – on the one hand and the subjective reason on the other hand, the first

> *dealing predominantly with the relation between means and ends, with the appropriateness of procedural rules in respect to the aims, which themselves are more or less accepted, without being questioned in terms of their own rationality.*

> *(Horkheimer, 1952: 5f.)*

(see as well the contribution on Science – Social Science – Practice Or: Searching for Responsibility in this volume). Saying this can be seen in some way as anthropological question, does not mean to deny a primarily social split going hand in hand, not least a division between powers:

those who could accumulate power and those who had been limited to a space of immediacy – only much later being translated into a systematic pattern of (i) separation of power as we find it in the modern state and (ii) a specific class structure: proprietors, labourers and managers.

Understanding this division as a principle feature is important – but we do not have to go further into detail of its epistemological meaning nor do we have to look at the social meaning in terms of the division of classes. The division has in its own terms only potential meanings in this respect and it had been a historical question of developing it further according to different options – and the relevance in various areas of societal life. I want to look at two points which are in my opinion frequently neglected – and it is from here where the general topic of this congress – Human Rights: For Sale or Saviour in the Globalising Market Economy – gains its very specific meaning. So, I want to talk about (i) the "outsourcing of economy" (and its later dominance) and (ii) the loss of rights in favour of gaining legal security. These are contemplations that are at the beginning, with which I enter a new area of thinking – and I want to invite you to follow in this attempt. And as new attempt, these considerations are at times possibly – and hopefully – provocative.

The Loss of the Economy

The world talks – and complains – about the economisation of life, the subordination of all fibres of social and individual existence under the economic interest. More correctly we hear people speaking about marketisation and managerialisation. Surely and justifiably, we can speak of such colonialisation. However, we may turn it around, looking at the origins, then speak of the loss of control over the economy by social forces, a process of outsourcing, leaving the economy to develop itself as special area, responsible for what had been understood as "wealth production". This is, of course, a complex development – we have to take into consideration the development of class structures, the question of property and control over the means of production etc; but I want to focus for a moment on two other issues: (i) the individualisation of economic actors, the meaning of products being already before the emergence of industrial capitalism only validated ex post, when they entered the market and the producers could verify the price of their products when they entered the exchange process (a development which peaked with the Renaissance) and (ii) reduction of wealth on its material dimension: the accumulation of goods. We can see the tension of the second in particular when we look at the early trade societies: the Fugger and Medici alike had been people who gathered huge amounts of material assets and still had to justify, legitimise this by supporting the fine arts, the beauty and joy of life. As questionable it is, we have to admit that in some way they "returned to society what they took out of society" – mind, I said as questionable as it is because much of this return was in reality just another way of personal gain in disguised form. – Anyway, that is a matter for another day and probably as well even for another public. Fact is that increasingly the development followed the pattern of separating individual life from social life. As part of this the accumulation of individual wealth, measured by success in econometric terms emerged as standard for well-being and success alike. Actually one may see here already that capitalism – in its infant stage – had been well compatible with Catholicism though it had been capitalism that finally forced into Protestantism, not only translating the fight for paradise into a fight for this-sidedness but also translating the fight for paradise into a fight for individual performance, expressed in individual well-being.

Of course, the decisive moment in this context is not the question of meaning or belief systems but the shift of the economic question away from its productive core towards circulation. Sure, it had been still the producer who had been required for success. However, not less important had been that measuring success had been increasingly seen as a matter of measuring success on the market place: measured ex ante. And the true entrepreneur had been the one who succeeded in what Marx later looked extensively at under the term of the exchange value. We are now dealing with the isolated individual, whose social existence is – evidently – only realised outside of the production and ex ante on the market: as matter of exchange. The social itself is redefined by actually de-socialising its character: rather than entering a social bond as productive relationship (and producing this relationship in the widest sense, going far beyond the production of commodities) it is now defined as (i) contractual relationship (ii) following in a highly segmented pattern.

The Loss of Rights

Speaking of a loss of rights is surely provocative – the increasing insistence on rights and moreover on equal rights for all had been not least a starring feature of Western enlightenment. And it is not least a contemporary accusation against for instance the Islam that it lacks a reformation on the basis of enlightenment. Surely, Tom M. Marshall's analysis is outstanding in tracing the development:

I shall call these three parts, or elements, civil, political and social. The civil element is composed of the rights necessary for individual freedom, liberty of the person, freedom of speech, thought and faith, the right to own property arid to conclude valid contracts, and the right to justice. The last is of a different order from the others, because it is the right to defend and assert all one's rights on terms of equality with others and by due process of law. This shows us that the institutions most directly associated with civil rights are the courts of justice. By the political element I mean the right to participate in the exercise of political power, as a member of a body invested with political authority or as an elector of the members of such a body. The corresponding institutions are parliament and councils of local government. By the social element I mean the whole range from the right to a modicum of economic welfare and security to the right to share to the full in the social heritage and to live the life of a civilised being according to the standards prevailing in the society. The institutions most closely connected with it are the educational system and the social services.

(Marshall, Tom H., 1950: 8)

However, there is another possible interpretation, seeing this development not as logical enhancement, the emergence of social rights from its predecessors. Instead, we may see it equally as reinvention of the social under the new conditions outlined by the revolution of the late 1700s and even the predecessor standing at the cradle of the renaissance. The conditions for the social changed fundamentally with the Renaissance: now it had to be developed on the foundation of a radically individualist account as it had been pointed out in the previous section: the "outsourcing of the economy" and the further development of its dominance as matter of objective reason. In simple terms, subsequent to the shift of the accumulation regime being geared to exchange processes rather than being focused on production, rights had to be translated into contracting relationships rather than dealing with the wider process of social production (on another occasion I am dealing with this question more in depth – see Herrmann, forthcoming). This means as well that contracts had been dealing with such segmented outcomes of social relationships rather than taking care of the permanent constitution of social relationships and rights. It may sound far-fetched but we can easily see in these patterns the deeper origin in what Niklas Luhmann called "Legitimation by Procedure" but as well some of the actual causes of the current crisis: the dis-embedding of the exchange process from their productive basis – later this will be taken up again.

'There is no such thing as society"

The phrase is well-known – at least to those who followed the political debates around the reign of the British Prime Minister Margaret Thatcher. The words in a little bit more context are as follows:

> *I think we have gone through a period when too many children and people have been given to understand "I have a problem, it is the Government's job to cope with it!" or "I have a problem, I will go and get a grant to cope with it!" "I am homeless, the Government must house me!" and so they are casting their problems on society and who is society? There is no such thing! There are individual men and women and there are families and no government can do anything except through people and people look to themselves first. It is our duty to look after ourselves and then also to help look after our neighbour and life is a reciprocal business and people have got the entitlements too much in mind without the obligations, because there is no such thing as an entitlement unless someone has first met an obligation and it is, I think, one of the tragedies in which many of the benefits we give, which were meant to reassure people that if they were sick or ill there was a safety net and there was help, that many of the benefits which were meant to help people who were unfortunate ...*

(Thatcher, 1987)

This statement had been correctly criticised by many, seeing in such statement as challenge to the social or welfare state, aiming on retrenchment policies.

However, as much as it had been a normative statement, arguing from a conservative, neo-liberal stance against possible claims of individuals against the state, it can be seen in a completely different light: as analytical statement that reflects very much the success of this neo-liberal strategy – the success of not only the recent historical retrenchment policies but the success of a secular movement of a radical individualisation and loss of deep-rooted socialbility.

In this light the retrenchment policies of the recent years are actually not as serious as they are frequently outlined – and though I do not want to follow up on this there are various studies showing that the actual level of provision is not necessarily worsening. The real problem has to be seen in the shift of the mode of regulation which makes now the individual – in different forms though – responsible: voucher systems, private insurance rather than public responsibility and others show different forms of desocialisation. This is highly relevant not least as matter of the re-definition of rights: it is underlining the shift to legalising rights on an individualist basis, following the rules of exchange rather than being a matter of "social production".

At the end this is characterising as well the social structures: class divisions not only disappear behind further differentiation: bourgeois and proletarian developing to owners, producers, managers; developing to various groups of stratifying systems: measuring various clusters and finally refusing to classify. In a way the individualisation of social rights – a contradiction in terms – may be taken as precise grasp of this development. It is the opposite to the Bismarkian extreme, who allegedly said that he would not know any classes anymore but only Germans – what came along as his justification to lead the world into a disastrous war is now the pure individualism (cf. as well Herrmann/Dorrity, 2009) that opens a way to a total social war – in which even the profiteer are potential losers.

We can now come back to what had been mentioned at the end of the previous section, the drift to "Legitimation by Procedure" and the dis-embedding of the exchange process from its productive basis as one of the actual causes of the current crisis.

The understanding of the social, being now reduced on exchange processes cannot deal anymore with the constitutional processes: the formulation of laws as technical process is more important than the political bargaining – a fact that can be seen in the accelerated speed of altering legislation: laws are not made to last but to fulfil short-term needs.

Paradoxically, the emphasis of norms like self-responsibility, mutual support, equality and dignity are loosing meaning as they are delinked from their context, namely their foundation in conditional relationships and constitutional processes, of which the factors are presented in the following table:

CONDITIONAL FACTORS	CONSTITUTIONAL FACTORS	NORMATIVE FACTORS
* socio-economic security * social cohesion * social inclusion * social empowerment	* personal security * social recognition * social responsiveness * personal capacity	* social justice (equity) * solidarity * democratic based citizenship * human dignity

Table 3

We can go a step further and say that any discussion on rights has to find its basis in real processes rather than looking out for normative guidelines – the self-evidence of the latter is misleading when it comes to complex processes.

Regaining the Commons – Regaining the Social

We can see many debates on the failures of the systems. Over the years – after 1917 – this system could actually grow and stabilise on the basis of competition. The socialist system on the one hand – whatever we think about it – had been one factor that paradoxically strengthened specifically its counterpart as the latter continued on the set parameters: individualist and econometric, short-term oriented growth.[61] Another factor of developing strength has to be seen in the ideological factor of the Balfour declaration – seemingly far out of context, but important as it put aside state building on the level of contracts rather than treaties.

But looking beyond this success we are now facing a massive crisis: the loss of socialism meant "paradise lost" – and in the present context the paradise is not the claimed paradise of the workers and peasants in the east nor the loss of an divine authoritative instance; rather it is the loss of the paradise of the free and social market economies of the west. And we find counter-movements. We can distinguish four major trends:

1) The radical market economies of the early phases – then at least in mainstream economics more or less uncontested, and on the advance on a global scale. A newly claimed universalist perspective of wealth. And although capitalism has created a single market, it did not erase the multiple divides between rich and poor: multiple divides as we find them within countries, between regions, between individuals and social groups and in very different aspects characterising people's life.

2) We find another trend, actually going very much hand in hand with this: the shift in the centre-periphery relationships and development of countries of the former periphery into new centres. It had been not least the before-mentioned development: the development of an unbridled capitalism that allowed this shift, giving now space for economic countries that had been up to hitherto at the periphery. On the global level it is the changing position of China in the global economy; and on a

---

[61] That the short-term orientation meant success in the long-term has to be seen as paradox though and we see today that long-term had been limited to the time of the ongoing competition.

smaller scale it had been Ireland for some time and it are the – temporarily failed – attempts of countries like Hungary to gain such special role. We should not overlook that for instance in Ireland these huge successes had been only possible by accepting paying huge social costs. And as well by accepting extreme consequences now – including schools asking the children to provide toilet paper (Irland, 2009).[62]

3) The – in my opinion not least – politically evoked celebration of vaguely new economics: if we look at the Nobel prize laureates in economics, we see a shift probably beginning with Amartya Sen, then going on to Joseph Stiglitz, Paul Krugman and as said now Elinor Ostrom and Oliver E. Williamson we see a shift towards a more open understanding of economics. In short, we see

- a turn towards political-economy, in tendency linking production, consumption as productive process, distribution and exchange and seeing them as entity
- a turn towards the "moralisation" of the economic process, seeing it based in and/or geared towards some kind of socio-moral responsibility
- a turn towards the economic process itself as one element of a wider process which can be taken as social process.

The development of awarding the Nobel Prize is surely not a feasible indicator. In my opinion the crucial point is anyway not really the shift towards a more Keynesian approach but the move towards a strengthened moral approach or an ethical economy. Indeed, we can see such moral dimension a long time before, actually marking the work of the two of the three greatest economists of modernity: Adam Smith and John Maynard Keynes – later I will get back to this, looking at the third one. But first briefly on Smith and Keynes. Everybody who at least briefly engaged in the work of the economist of Scottish enlightenment will know well the Inquiry into the Nature and Causes of the Wealth of Nations; and will be equally aware of The Theory of Moral Sentiments. And the economist who pleaded for new policies as answer on the world economic crisis in the 1920s is not only known for his General Theory of Employment, Interest and Money. But he is equally known for his general reformist notion:

---

[62] Sure, looking at another article, written by Julia Bönisch under the heading Gebühren für Schultoiletten (Bönisch, Julia, 2009) it seems to be worthwhile to make a comparative study on schools and toilets in Europe.

The day is not far off when the economic problem will take the back seat where it belongs, and the arena of the heart and the head will be occupied or reoccupied, by our real problems / the problems of life and of human relations, of creation and behavior and religion.

(Keynes, John Maynard, 1945-1946)

And it is not only about such very basic moral considerations, but it is also about the more concrete questions. Again and again we find at least since the 1970 social indicator movements; we find as well the debates on well-being and the search for European economic policies which should not be an end in itself but contribute to the living standards of European citizens. And more recently we find this merging into a debate under the heading "Beyond GDP", the recent outcome being a communication issued by the European Commission under the title GDP and Beyond. Measuring Progress in a Changing World (European Commission, 2009).

In any case, there are two problems with these searches: The first question is from where can we actually gain the moral values that we claim as guiding principles? The second question concerns a more pragmatic issue: The current approaches of going beyond GDP lack a clear focus. They surely take into account very important issues but there is no clarity about their order and there is only intuitive consideration from where they come.

This brings us possibly to the more fundamental shift which is only partly reflected in the list of Nobel laureates. It is about the very inclusion of more complex patterns of policy making as well into the economic realm, though remaining with the arguments fundamentally within the framework of a divided economy, namely an economic system which separates rather strictly between production in the strict sense, consumption, distribution and exchange.

4) The search for niches – alternative economies, sometimes looking for an alternative globalisation, sometimes seeing themselves as anti-globalisation movements. It is a quit diverse field, often contradicting in terms. For instance we find a claim for a social economy though is brought forward with the knowledge that it can only be maintained in a small niche and by a small number of especially conscious people, hoping that it may spread further from there. Nothing is wrong with such approaches though the problem remains that the social character is at least limited in scope if not as well in terms of the actual understanding of the social: the danger is simply the limitation of strategies on

temporary solutions within a limited space of action, lacking structural effects. In this sense they are depending on individual will, rather than on structural change.

Who? What? How?

At the beginning I pointed on two questions: Who are we? And: What kind of alternatives do we look for? We could leave them open for a while – and still, they are at the core of any consideration if it wants to be a serious consideration. And they actually underlie – unspoken – the analysis. And finally another question has to be added: How can we get there?

I am well aware of the limitations of the following remarks. The critical points of any strategy are the following:

- I see a flaw in orientations on moral approaches and also in approaches that are reduced on calls for (re-)regulation – this is concerned with both, dealing with the challenges from the economic crisis and the questions of human rights.

- I see a fundamental problem with the outsourcing of economic processes and their separation from wider aspects that go beyond the production of goods and monetary values.

- I propose that any solution to rights and economic crisis – as interrelated challenge – has to look for ways of including global and long-term time perspectives.

- I think we need to think about possibilities not as technical but as substantial question, acknowledging the context of space and time.

This may sound abstract – but actually it is rather simple and can easily be translated into some policy requirements with which I want to conclude. And I know that some of these topics will be taken up during the following negotiations of this conference.

1) On the first issue: we need to overcome the limitations of the abstract character of moral norms and formal criteria. For achieving this, we need to present a clear focus, i.e. a clear understanding of the kind of society and the kind of living together we want to achieve. Though it may sound to be a circular argument, we have to develop our thinking from everyday's life and therein

the extent to which people are able to participate in social relationships under conditions which enhance their well-being, capacity and individual potential.

(Beck et al. 2007: 25)

This gives a clear orientation to any policy – be it social policy or economic policy, policies in the areas of health care or education: it is the need to approach political questions from a vision of the society we want to live in.

This provides as well a sound framework for looking at specific issues as for instance technological innovations, the globalisation of economic processes or demographic change. However, the more important aspect is the inclusion of an implicit wider understanding of processes in question. As much as we are usually confronted with a limitation of economic processes on their econometric dimension and the institutional mechanisms as means of steering we have now a different access as well towards institutions: Politics matter, indeed. And we see this not least in the different patterns applied for instance in the member states of the European Union, thus in a relatively small and somewhat homogenous space. The institutional differences are actually much more important in their meaning of mechanisms of socialisation rather than simply as matter of regulation. This is clearly shown when looking for instance at the Nordic countries and their relative success in answering the different economic crisis. This is surely about economic performances and the "gains of having productive social policy". But here it is proposed to see it as matter of a relatively extended degree of socialised processes that include economic mechanisms in a wider understanding.

2) Though societies are highly differentiated, this does not mean that we can reduce complexity by concentrating on segments of societies: bureaucracy exists because it does not follow the abstract rules as outlined by Max Weber; the market economy works only where interventions guarantee that the mechanisms that are immanently undermining the market principle are counteracted. And society does not work as invisible hand, steering egoistic rational action. It is about the social existence of humans, producing their existence in society, the action being based on the interrelationship of conditional, constitutional and normative factors, as tentatively outlined in the following figure.

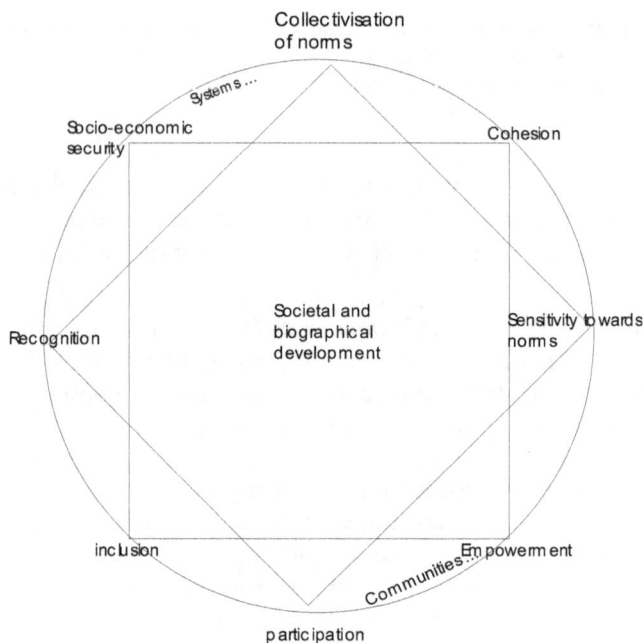

Collectivisation
of norms

Systems ...

Socio-economic
security

Cohesion

Societal and
biographical
development

Recognition

Sensitivity towards
norms

inclusion

Empowerment

Communities...

participation

Figure 11

This opens – actually requires – to look at economic processes as matter of socio-economy, emphasising and bringing together

- socio-economics as matter of accumulation regimes and modes of regulations
- social economy
- social rights as globalising the orientation of the first in terms of space ("global social justice")
- social rights as globalising the orientation of the first in terms of time ("sustainability").

3) Looking at material living standards and well-being is, of course, indispensable. However, for analysing the real dimension of this it may be required to shift the attention: Rather than going beyond GDP we should look at other than GPD, namely the "production of social integrity".

4) The fourth point is surely the most difficult – looking for the actors, looking for the practice perspective. I cannot look at even all major points that play a role here. I only want to mention two. (i) I mentioned

Smith and Keynes – and then I pointed on a third economist, then without saying his name. Of course, the person who had been referred to is Karl Marx. I do not want to dispute the political meaning here – at least we are back to a stage where it is again allowed to name him without being blamed. I want to point on the epistemological dimension of his work and even here looking at one point only – a factor that is in my opinion of central importance in the context of our discussion. Already in his earlier considerations, before writing his opus magnum The Capital, he elaborated the entity of production, consumption, distribution and exchange. And he emphasised the need to concentrate on production as a complex process, going far beyond the production of commodities. If we look closely, we can say it had been not least about the production of rights (see in this context the contribution "Rights-Based Approaches Against Social Injustice – Putting Social Law into Perspective" in this volume).

(ii) Finally, let us not forget what brought us here on these two days: we are gathering here on the occasion of the 100th anniversary of the Finish Social Policy Association. This should remind us that we went a long way: hazardous at times, being crisscrossed by many failures – and as diverse as they had been if looking at the single cases: what all these stoppages had been about, they have in common that they failed to work on visions, only engaging in the search for technical solutions for short-term problems, only being concerned with comparison of good practice rather then looking for a society in which people have rights as social beings rather than as individualised subjects of competitive markets.

References

Beck, W./van der Maesen, L./Walker, A. (eds.) (2007) Chapter 3: "Theoretical Foundations", for forthcoming third book on social quality. The Hague: Foundation for Social Quality

Bönisch, Julia, 2009: Gebühren für Schultoiletten – Kleine Geschäfte, große Geschäfte; in: Sueddeutsche Zeitung; 24.09.2009, 9:15 (http://www.sueddeutsche.de/jobkarriere/291/487694/text/ - 19/10/2009 6:48 a.m.

European Commission, 2009: Communication from the Commission to the Council and the European Parliament: GDP and beyond. Measuring progress in a changing world; Brussels, 20.8.2009; COM(2009) 433 final

Herrmann, Peter: 2009: Gemeinschaft der Gesellschaft – die Suche nach einem Definitionsrahmen für Prekarität; in: Hepp, Rolf (ed.): The Fragilisation of Socio-structural Components/Die Fragilisierung soziostruktureller Komponenten; Bremen: Europaeischer Hochschulverlag; 2009: 76-107

Herrmann, Peter, forthcoming: Searching for Global Policy

Herrmann, Peter/Dorrity, Claire, 2009: Critique of Pure Individualism; in: Dorrity, Claire/Herrmann, Peter [eds.]: Claire Dorrity: Social Professional Activity – The Search for a Minimum Common Denominator in Difference; New York: Nova Science

Horkheimer, Max, 1952: Der Begriff der Vernunft. Festrede bei der Rektoratsübergabe der Johann Wolfgang Goethe-Universität am 20. November 1951; in: Frankfurter Universitätsreden, Heft 7; Frankfurt/M.: Vittorio Klostermann: 5-17

Irland, 2009: Ireland. Mit dem eigenen Klopapier zur Schule; in: Sueddeutsche Zeitung; 07.10.2009, 13:50; http://www.sueddeutsche.de/,ra711/jobkarriere/785/490165/text/ - 19/10/2009 6:44 a.m.

Keynes, John Maynard, 1945-1946: First Annual Report of the Arts Council; quoted on: http://en.wikiquote.org/wiki/John_Maynard_Keynes - 19/10/2009 7:26 a.m.

Marshall, Tom H., 1950: Citizenship and Social Class; in: Citizenship and Social Class; Marshall, Tom H./Tom Bottomore; London et altera: Pluto Press1992

Thatcher, Margaret, 1987: "Aids, education and the year 2000!"; Interview for Woman's Own; Douglas Keay, Woman's Own; 31 October: 8-10; http://www.margaretthatcher.org/speeches/displaydocument.asp?docid=106689 - 19/10/2009 6:30 a.m.

Multilevel Governance – Participatory Democracy and Civil Society's Role in Governance in the Perspective of the Lisbon Treaty

Notes in Preparation of an Address to the NGO-Forum 2009 in Örebro, Sweden; October 2009

It seems to be a quantum leap: from seeing Switzerland with rather unique mechanisms of direct democracy as outsider of European political culture – in many cases being even ridiculed for what was seen as oddity – to the European Union, now stating in the potential Treaty (Council of the European Union, 2008):

> *In order to promote good governance and ensure the participation of civil society, the Union institutions, bodies, offices and agencies shall conduct their work as openly as possible.*

(15:1)

And this is understood as demand that

> *[t]he institutions shall maintain an open, transparent and regular dialogue*

(11)

There are other relevant messages in the Treaty when it comes to participatory democracy– not least the one on the citizen's initiative which allows the people to be pro-actors of policies, i.e. demanding the commission in a referendum to get active (11.4 with reference to 24).

On the one hand I do not want to enter into this debate – I think it is a rather specific one; nor do I want to enter into the debate on something that may cause deep hesitation to even go further in thinking about participation in the framework of the Treaty – the fact of an inflation. The term participation occurs 54 times in the Treaty, we can find the term participate 38 times. And one can surely ask then if there isn't the danger of participation loosing any real meaning.

Leaving this inflation aside there is another issue that can be seen as ground for being in very principal terms sceptical. Article 10:3 reads

> *3. Every citizen shall have the right to participate in the democratic life of the Union. Decisions shall be taken as openly and as closely as possible to the citizen.*

(10:3)

It marks the tension between representative democracy as it is laid down in Article 10.1. and the claims of participatory democracy – a tension that has to be seen as hugely important for all attempts of participatory democracy going hand in hand with representative principles. It is a simple logical tension: by such introduction the principle of representation is itself questioned and we find a paradoxical tension of following kind:

representative

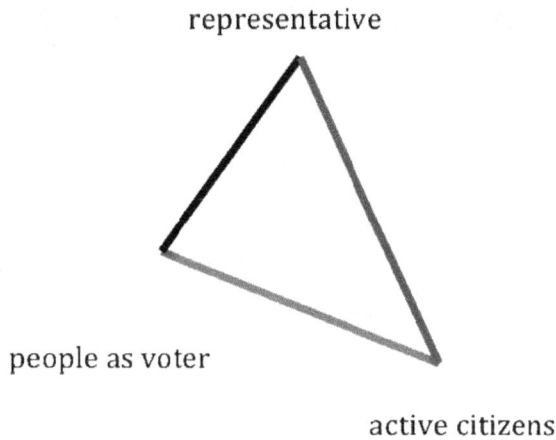

people as voter

active citizens

Figure 12

Leaving the very principal difficulties aside, there are interesting features that are in particular ways linked with the fact of multilevel governance as it is seen specifically in the EU-context.

First, the general pattern is a shift from governing to governance – this seems to be a secular trend, opening more space for directly including citizens into the process of preparing, making and implementing decision. It is important to highlight that governance is to some extent a matter of differentiation and changing the feature of the state or statutory system – to some extent only consciously and pronouncedly separating between different phases of a process:

Decisions			
preparing: ventilating needs	planning	deciding	Implementing

Figure 13

Second, in general we are now dealing not only with different levels of reference but – so the claim and envisaged architecture – with the direct and conscious interaction of and intervention in cross-level-governance.

	local			regional			national			supranational		
Preparing												
Planning												
Deciding												
Implementing												

Figure 14

Third, we still have to get to a final feature of this pattern, namely the conscious integration of citizens into the architecture.

		local			regional			national			supranational		
	citizen	NGO	institution	c	n	i	c	n	i	c	n	i
Preparing												
Planning												
Deciding												
Implementing												

Figure 15

Any further attempt to present this in some visual form goes beyond capacity and it seems to be sufficient at this stage to bring forward a provocation: the debate is to a large extent jeopardised by the traditional understanding of participation. Strictly speaking the term goes back to the Latin language and translates from pars capere into taking part. This is quite different to what we get when looking at synonyms – they lead us for instance to contributing, input and sharing. For me such a shift from tribuere to capere – from giving to taking – seems to be quite remarkable.

So, it may be worthwhile as well to look primarily at what we actually do and can contribute and how we fit into the entire system of governance.

– One remark seems to be necessary before we move further: governance, seemingly a new pattern in policy-making, is in my view not really new. New is at most the structured and conscious way of dealing with processes of governance and then the attempt to look at these processes by way of applying some strict and systematic measures, as they had been outlined in the White Paper on Governance, published by the European Commission in 2001 (European Commission, 2001). These are coming across under five "Principles of Good Governance", namely

- Openness
- Participation
- Accountability
- Effectiveness
- Coherence

(ibid., 10)

Now, I will look mainly at the following questions:

1) Who wants to take part by contributing? – And being at the NGO-Forum means of course to look for a more positive definition of NGOs and civil society of which they are part.

2) To what and by which means can such contribution be undertaken?

3) What are the expectations of such contributions?

4) Finally, what is needed to contribute in this way?

Let me briefly state from where I am coming: having worked for a long time in advocacy and political groups I got involved in academic work on the Third Sector while working on my PhD and later when I had been looking for "something new", searching for a field for my academic work – this had been in the 1980, the question of European social policy emerging as a rather thing stripe at the horizon and the field of NGOs only a tiny, really marginal moment of this stripe. Academic work needs practice; and it needs this especially when it comes to – at the time – such an exotic field. So I got in touch and got involved in building up what now seems to be a strong European civil society. I had been involved in various positions and roles and can probably say with some reason that I know the development from within, and at the same time continuing from this perspective research on this topic. Probably not as academic as the work of some of my colleagues in the academic world – as they undertook the blueprint empirical work, not always having a foot close into the door. And not as pragmatic as some of my colleagues in the NGOs who had been facing the day-to-day challenges and their permanent threats and opportunities.

1) Who?

Answering this question can be kept brief – though there are of course several academic discourses which raise complex questions about individual organisations, specific types and finally as well the "sector". This debate does not deserve further discussion here. Important is to maintain a wide understanding and in particular to look at the historical dimension. A crucial point is that we are in various regards confronted with a movement rather with organisations in the strict sense. Of course, in today's terms the focus is quite naturally on organisations, for instance in the understanding of the John-Hopkins Comparative Nonprofit Sector Project, defining them by five "features" and two "restrictions". Relevant organisations had been characterised by some formal structures, their private, i.e. non-governmental character, not being profit-distributing, self-governing and voluntary; furthermore they had been considered as non-religious and non-political (see for instance Salamon/Anheier, 1994; 13-15).

This definition had been as well accepted as guiding the first EU-official document, dealing with the topic, published by the European Commission in 1995 (European Commission, 1995). However, looking historically at these organisations it is obvious that they emerged in different respects as processes against rigid structures. In very broad terms we can see them as externalised parts of the increasingly institutionalised capitalist market – as a kind of counterpoint; and we can see this as well reflected in their interpretation as countering market failure on the one hand and state failure on the other hand. It is important to highlight this historical background in order to maintain a dynamic understanding that goes beyond a structuralist approach.

In this respect a tiny detail appears to be interesting: the European Commission's document from 1995 can be found on the website of the DG enterprise. It is worthwhile to mention it and just to think for a second about it. Is it a matter of usurpation? Or is it a matter of acknowledging the important economic role? Or even a matter of redefining the economy, acknowledging its wider meaning?

2) Where and How?

Keeping this in mind we can easily see that any contribution is in particular geared towards the interface. It must appear somewhat strange that we find on the one hand a certain negative sense of the sector: non-profit and non-governmental. The frequently used term third sector may be more helpful, expressing that it is a sector that allows the development of some kind of fortitude for the entire system. It is about allowing the other sectors functioning with a limited logic or rationality. This implies on the one hand a limitation of the sector as much as it is itself characterised by a specific particularism; and it is about the sectors standing as acting as complementing force. This is only to some extent grasped if we look at the negative side (non-profit and non-governmental). It is as well about the fact that the relevant organisations play a positive role in maintaining some kind of completing function. Such function can mean taking over certain soci(et)ally necessary functions that are otherwise neglected; or it can mean to act as vanguard or advocate. This means that these organisations are not defined by their negativity but by the positive role they play in society.

However, we have to be careful. Positive is not meant to provide an assessment in terms of values: many of these organisations are "negative": we find racist movements as well as we find extremely conservative organisations with respect to equal opportunities and many others could be added. However, the "positive" aspect is about their function. For this we have to consider that these organisations are in one or another way result of a process of differentiation. They fulfil functions that broke away from other parts within society – seemingly we return to the negative definition. However, the difference is that we actually do not start at all from characterising these organisations or the sector. Instead, we start from looking at society at large and located within a concrete society the role of different actors, in this context the organisations and movements in question. This entails possible conflicts and tensions and has nothing to do with any valuation.

3) Expected Outcome

One of the central – or even the central – outcome is usually seen in two factors: (i) We find major service providers organised as NGOs; (ii) NGOs contribute to democracy and foster democratic values.

Let me be at least a little bit provocative on these two points – with respect to the first factor I want to say that the organisations in question are not service providers but in some way the major undermining factor when it comes to service provision – and we can see this as a positive factor. Where we find strong NGOs in form of self-help groups, in form of civil society movements, as matter of informal support networks where social services in the strict sense – as professional services – are actually not needed. Or they are at least not needed in the same extensive way as they would be otherwise. Paradoxically: they make professional services much more needs-oriented than they would be without such networks.

Coming to the second point, I dare to say that they are not contributing to democracy. It is more to see them as "democracy itself". Democracy is today commonly seen as representative democracy – and there is surely good reason to refer to such a system as it is not least based on the separation of power. However, we have to see as well that with this emerging new state and society of the modern world we enter a world which is characterised by two rather fundamental tensions: the one being the tension between society and state, the other being the tension between the economy and its civil 'counterpart'.

We can come back to the unequal triangle from above which looks in its more basic from like the following:

state

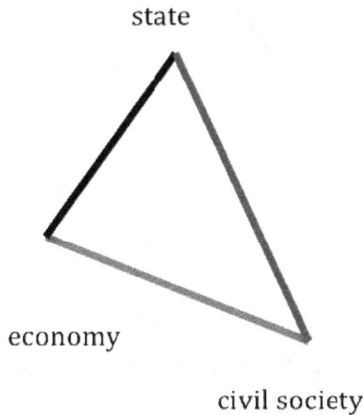

economy

civil society

Figure 16

This had never been an equal-sided triangle as the link between economy and state had been much stronger than the one between state and civil society.

A large part of the problematique can be seen in the fact that in today's world even the voting system is, if not a market itself so to a large extent depending on the economic standing. It is in its simplification the competition for votes – indeed on a market where votes are exchanged against promises of performance, of benefits for the voter rather voting for somebody who is truly representing interests in a wider contest of different societal powers. Such system is hardly geared towards a general interest. Rather, particularism is paradoxically not least a matter that is maintained in this "representative system" – and the critique is not so much directed towards the three agents – market, state and civil society. Rather it is geared towards the fact of the braking points between the three corners, each corner being caught in the limited array of self-maintenance. The result is easily a relationship of domination by which the economy gains the role of being basis and superstructure at the same time (as we see it in particular in current politics: the domination of neo-liberal actors from the economic side over the other players which can take rather different forms[63]).

economy

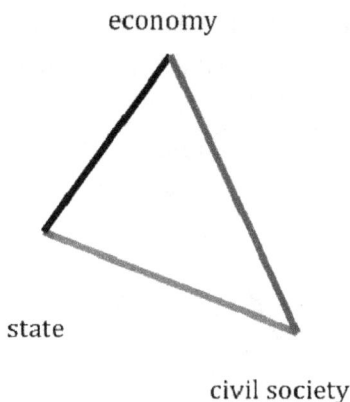

state

civil society

Figure 17

Or: a chaotic system of different players, characterised by situational advantages and lack of strategic planning –

---

[63] This may be just a matter of suppression but it may be also a matter of subordination but adaptation, as we can see it for instance in the managerialist approaches to equality or the profitable orientation on environmental topics.

Figure 18

– And I leave it to you to decide which symbol stands for which agent – and one may even ask oneself if there any fixed attribution of roles actually does exist.

Figure 19

4) Required Framework

So far we had been to a large extent caught within a holy trinity – and I want to propose to overcome the limitation of this approach, now looking at the requirements for participatory democracy. It should be clear from the outset: (i) participatory democracy cannot and should not even try to replace representative democracy – and it is even problematic to speak of a complementary role. It is as complementary as potatoes are complementary to apples – the French language may propose a close relationship between the two but we should not be tempted to follow the simple terminological proposition. This, of course, equally forbids seeing them as opposites like hell and heaven, as the one is growing above the ground, the other beneath and in the soil. Thinking complementarities is difficult – but we cannot get away with forcing complex questions into straightjackets. (ii) And we should not allow ourselves falling into the trap of looking for too much institutional safeguard. As important as that is, it is of crucial importance to recognise that a decisive moment of these organisations and movements is by definition their localisation somewhat outside of the system. In particular as long as we maintain the unequal relative strength and the disjointing of the economy from society and the separation between state and demos, we have to face the fact of a severe tension.

Thus I propose not to look primarily at a "just space for NGOs in an unjust world". Instead we should claim a more substantial shift that acknowledges the need not least of regaining of a demos.

Commonly demos simply refers to the (ordinary) people of a commonality of the ancient Greek state.

If we take this as point of departure we can see the need for a shift as well in the currently only emerging debate on participatory democracy. Democracy has to be brought back to its substance, substance being defined as essential nature. And this is not primarily about processes of decision-making. Rather, we have to put something else at the core of democracy: the social as being geared to enhance

> the extent to which people are able to participate in social relationships under conditions which enhance their well-being, capacity and individual potential
>
> (Beck et al. 2007: 25)

Now we can leave the trinity behind and move towards a more fruitful approach that allows looking at the organisations in question not as one sector defining and defending own orientations and rights. Instead, we face now a sector that contributes very specifically to social quality in the understanding just outlined.

Figure 20

Actually this view on conditional factors should be complemented by a set of constitutional and normative factors, all shown together in the following overview:

CONDITIONAL FACTORS	CONSTITUTIONAL FACTORS	NORMATIVE FACTORS
* socio-economic security	* personal security	* social justice (equity)
* social cohesion	* social recognition	* solidarity
* social inclusion	* social responsiveness	* democratic based citizenship
* social empowerment	* personal capacity	* human dignity

Figure 21

Taking this together, it means not least that we are able to overcome the residual role when it comes to defining the "third sector".

Important is that we have now a focus towards we can relate the different actors and activities. Making a further step away from thinking in the triangular model we may try to contemplate on different sets of "open concentric circles":

- One set would be located in the four corners of the factors, looking for the contribution of different actors – but as well the opportunities to contribute.

---

[64] Taken from the website of the European Foundation of Social Quality: ww.socialquality.org

159

The actual question would be: To which extent do and can actors contribute to socio-economic security etc.? And furthermore: in which way do and can different actors contribute (the latter requiring the "open circles". For instance are business organisations surely "closer" to economic issues. However, this does not mean that economic activities or activities securing the socio-economic status are not relevant when it comes to NGOs or civil society organisations. – Cum grano salis, this can be examined for the different factors.

- An entirely different set would be oriented towards the centre, looking at the contribution of the different agents to "the social" and its quality.

  The question then would be around the role played towards integrating the different factors. Are agents "remaining in their corner" or are they are actually linking the different poles? In which way are they actively contributing to the further development of the social by actually allowing people to actively engage in and influence their social being rather than forcing them into socially isolated roles?

This can have very different dimensions and I do only want to mention a few points which are in my view crucially important when it comes to multilevel governance and the EU.

1.) Mutuality seems to be an issue that is at the centre in three ways.

* On the one side the further shift of policymaking away from the local and national level means that we face a need for maintaining identity. This is increasingly difficult (and can be seen in the "precarious, free-floating individual of postmodernity"), but on the other hand it requires the manageable space in which action is taken and decisions are prepared. The "democratic deficit" is not least a deficit of recognising local policies – the needs and their recognition on the central level. His goes far beyond the need of institutional reforms on the central level. And I am sure that there is more to be done to make the Open Method of Coordination really working. The reason is quite simple: from what we know from the different member states, the democratic process actually barely reaches really the level of "every day's life of ordinary people".

* On the other side we find needs of creating new mutuality. We can see this most clearly when it comes to specific groups which build some new kinds of solidarities and mutual support systems, I think of special

importance are here – for obvious reasons – young people and, to the extent to which resources can be secured, people living in poverty.

* Furthermore, the interpenetration of economics by radical neo-liberalist politics had a counter-effect, namely the strengthening of some germs of an alternative economic policy. The social economy – for many without doubt part of the organisations we are looking at – could enter certain areas and actually changed at least some orientations of the economic system as well. We should not underestimate the role of various European programs actually supporting civil society organisations by taking such stances (of course, a major problem being that these usually remain being outsiders).

2.) A real challenge can be seen in the process of regaining and maintaining proximity. Usually this is seen as matter of civil society organisations providing proximity services. This is surely one point. But another point is that these actors are able to establish proximity. If we speak of a democratic deficit it is usually considered as lack of appropriate institutional mechanisms. What I would see as more important is the lack of this kind of proximity: the emergence of a people, a demos.

In this respect it is simply necessary (i) to foster civil society as bearer or expression of such demos; but (ii) it is necessary as well to refine civil society, not allowing it to stand outside as "third sector" but fostering the attention to truly holistic approaches – not as matter of personalities but also in terms of societies. This requires not least as well a thorough consideration of economics and of the true challenges of multilevel policies. As important as it is to utilise in this case appropriate instruments as e.g. the open method of coordination, the real challenge is to bring the Community Method in the widest understanding down to the ground. It may be – and hopefully is – a little bit provocative: as important as it is to get a voice of civil society heard in Brussels, it is more important to make the European ears listen to civil societies on the ground: where every day's life can be found and where it is not divided between economic, political and civil life but where it is concerned about the overall social quality of being.

Where to Go? – Theses for Proposing an Outlook

First

Paradoxically, re-localisation of policies means to Europeanise politics. Mind the double meaning: The localisation of politics is currently extremely difficult. Recently, being confronted with the Manifesto of the Spring Alliance, José Manuel Barroso apparently expressed his support, however, stating that any progress would be blocked by the unwillingness of the member states. However, we probably all remember cases where on the member state level the EU had been accused not to allow certain policies which would have been favoured from their side. The problem is that probably both sides are wrong. If we look at academic analysis we find complex patterns as opting out possibilities, package deals, co-decision procedures et altera. The actual problem is that it is not clear who is responsible – so in this sense it is necessary to locate the responsible entities. The current pattern does not allow any clear decision – and in turn it means that general frameworks are developed, perforated and watered down by exemptions, exceptions, adaptations etc.. Even the Treaty as it stands currently for ratification is characterised by about 37 protocols, 50 general declarations and 15 declarations by the member states – thus by a huge amount of exceptions even in respect to the EU's most general framework. Another point in question is that the lack of a clear localisation subsequently leads to the lack of power of the legislative institutions and the gain of power of the jurisdiction. Overcoming such a lack of clarity would mean locating responsibility. And it is such a process that would actually allow relocating policies in the understanding of its applicability on the local level.

Second

This has to be explained – not least as this is not an automatic mechanism. It can only work if the gained clarity is complemented by strict accountability. The problem with this principle is that accountability is by no means a question of formal accountability. At the centre is the need to establish a link between the demos. Being accountable to a demos – as said: (ordinary) people of a commonality – means that expertise has to be developed not as matter of knowledge about legal details and technical questions of implementation. This clearly defines the need to closely link to people's everyday's life. And this is to be found for instance in spatially defined communities, in certain groups that organise themselves across borders along lines of specific interests or gatherings on the basis of demographic or physical characters.

Third

In this sense the open method of coordination actually could have allowed to make huge progress: bringing in a loop of permanent feedbacks, i.e. EU-plans, local expertise and strategic policy-making. However, how it actually works is problematic: due in particular to a lack of obligation of member states to follow real processes of consultation.

Fourth

We are back to field one: The need of localisation. Currently, policy making lacks to a large extent accountability: if something happens or if it doesn't is not of central importance. It seems that the muddling through of contemporary systems is largely grounded on two principles. (i) the Mathew principle according to which somebody else can be blamed; and (ii) the emergency- principle: needed is action only when it is actually too late (as previously clearly shown with the debate ion the Constitution and the later Plan D). Political action has to be accountable also in the sense of having consequences for forbearing doing the necessary.

Fifth

Not least, it means: NGOs should not primarily look for ways to enter the institutions. Nor should they look for providing "better services" in the sense of increasing their competitiveness. On the contrary: NGOs should see it as at least equally important to force politicians out of the institutions as laws may be made inside but rights are negotiated outside (see in this context Herrmann, forthcoming); and to show that democracy is not about votes but about daily life; and that services are not about competition but about social quality.

References

Beck, W., van der Maesen, L. & Walker, A. (eds.) (2007) Chapter 3: "Theoretical Foundations", for forthcoming third book on social quality. The Hague: Foundation for Social Quality

Council of the European Union, 2008: Council of the European Union: Consolidated versions of the Treaty on European Union and the Treaty on the functioning of the European Union, as they will result from the amendments introduced by the Treaty of Lisbon, signed on 13 December 2007 in Lisbon; Brussels, 30 April 2008; ref. 6655/1/08 REV 1

European Commission, 1995: Promoting the Role of Voluntary Organisations and Foundations in Europe; Communication from the Commission; EN/23/95/00891100.W00 (EN); http://ec.europa.eu/enterprise/library/lib-social_economy/orgfd_en.pdf- 01/11/2009 6:59 a.m.

European Commission, 2001: White Paper European Governance; Brussels, July 2001; COM(2001) 428, July 2001; http://eur-lex.europa.eu/LexUriServ/site/en/com/2001/com2001_0428en01.pdf - 13/10/2009 4:21 p.m.)

Salamon, Lester M./Anheier, Helmut K., 1994: The Emerging Sector. An Overview, 1994

About the Author

dr. phil (Bremen, Germany). Studies in Sociology (Bielefeld, Germany), Economics (Hamburg), Political Science (Berlin) and Social Policy and Philosophy (Bremen). Had been teaching at several Third Level Institutions across the EU; currently correspondent to the Max Planck Institute for Foreign and International Social Law (Munich, Germany), senior advisor to the European Foundation on Social Quality (Amsterdam, Netherlands) and Advisory Board of EURISPES – Instituto di Studi Politici, Economici e Sociali, Rome, member of the Scientific Board of ATTAC – Association pour la taxation des transactions financières pour l'aide aux citoyens and Associate Member of the Eurasian Center for Big History and System Forecasting at the Moscow State University.

Director of the Independent Research Institute European Social, Organisational and Science Consultancy (Aghabullogue, Ireland) and teaching at the University College of Cork, Department of Applied Social Studies, (Cork, Ireland), where he holds the position of an adjunct senior lecturer and Kuopion Yliopisto, Yhteiskuntatieteellinen tiedekunta. Sosiaalipolitiikan ja sosiaalipsykologian laitos (Kuopio, Finland), where he is adjunct professor. He held various positions as visiting professor and is currently in this position at the Corvinus University in Budapest.

Member of several editorial boards; editor of the book series Applied Social Studies – Recent Developments, International and Comparative Perspectives (New York, USA) and Studies in Comparative Pedagogies and International Social Work and Social Policy (Bremen, Germany); peer-reviewing for several journals in the social area and book series.

www.ingramcontent.com/pod-product-compliance
Lightning Source LLC
Chambersburg PA
CBHW032144020426
42334CB00016B/1220